Contents

Going to

WITHDRAWN

Trial

A Step-by-Step Guide to Trial
Practice and Procedure

Second Edition

Daniel I. Small, Editor

ABA **General Practice, Solo and Small Firm Section
American Bar Association**

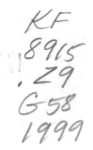
Cover design by Gray Cat Graphic Design.

All trademarks are property of their respective owners.

The materials contained herein represent the opinions of the authors and editors and should not be construed to be the action of either the American Bar Association or the General Practice, Solo and Small Firm Section unless adopted pursuant to the bylaws of the Association.

Nothing contained in this book is to be considered as the rendering of legal advice for specific cases, and readers are responsible for obtaining such advice from their own legal counsel. This book and any forms and agreements herein are intended for educational and informational purposes only.

10 09 08 07 06   8 7 6 5 4

Small, Daniel I., 1954-
    Going to trial / Daniel I. Small. -- 2nd ed.
        p. cm.
    Includes bibliographical references and index.
    ISBN 1-57073-723-1
    1. Trial practice--United States Outlines, syllabi, etc.
  I. Going to trial. II. Title.
  KF8915.Z9G58 1999
    347.73'504--dc21   99-37774
                                                              CIP

Discounts are available for books ordered in bulk. Special consideration is given to state bars, CLE programs, and other bar-related organizations. Inquire at Book Publishing, ABA Publishing, American Bar Association, 321 N. Clark Street, Chicago, Illinois 60610.

www.abanet.org/abapubs

Summary of Contents

Preface

The first edition of *Going to Trial: A Step-by-Step Guide to Trial Practice and Procedure*, was published in 1984 and became the all-time best seller for the ABA's General Practice, Solo and Small Firm Section (GPSSF). It was a sentinel book, overwhelmingly well received because it did an excellent job, according to its many readers, of laying out the preparations for trial. In this new edition of *Going to Trial*, Dan Small has culled the best of the first edition, added substantially to it, and created a superb new reference tool to help today's lawyers improve their trial practice, whether they go to court weekly or once a year.

A lot has changed during the last 15 years. In 1984, lawyers could not foresee legal issues that would be raised by such things as terrorism in the United States, A.I.D.S., cameras in the courtroom, the Internet, or Presidential indiscretions. We could not guess at how common summary trials, private trials, and alternate dispute resolution would become, nor know about the increased demands on our support staff , or even that we would be seeing more litigious clients. And we could only dream of the technology that is now available to every lawyer.

Despite these changes and many others, the steps to preparing for trial are essentially the same as they have always been. Every trial lawyer must do a thorough job of discovery, handle depositions deftly, pick jurors carefully, and deal with the myriad details associated with every case. That will never change.

Dan Small has brought *Going to Trial* forward 15 years so that it can help you prepare for trial today. The chapters correspond to major steps in trying a case, from initial interview through closing argument, but the book now includes sections on technology and jury selection and provides a selection of core documents that can make every lawyer's case flow more smoothly. And there are plenty of tips, sample forms, checklists, questionnaires, agreements, and letters to supplement the text. The samples are flexible enough to be adapted to many legal situations, and can be instantly accessed on the diskettes that are included with this new edition.

Dan Small was the perfect person to handle the enormous task of updating and revising *Going to Trial* and he did an outstanding job. He is a partner in a busy trial practice in Boston, has been a Federal prosecutor, and taught trial advocacy. He is also an arbitrator for the American Arbitration

Association, vice-chair of the Committee on White Collar Crime for the Section of Criminal Justice, and appears frequently on national television as a legal commentator. As if that were not enough, Dan is a prolific author and has written numerous articles for newspapers, magazines, and books about litigation. His latest book, *Preparing Witnesses*, has been a bestseller for GPSSF since it published in July 1998.

It is our sincere belief that the second edition of *Going to Trial* is a necessity for any lawyer facing litigation today or in the decade to come. We are indebted to Dan Small for giving so generously of his time, and to his family for forgiving his absence while he was working on the book.

Eunice Clavner
Publications Board Chair
General Practice, Solo and Small Firm Section

Acknowledgments

Working on one book that encompasses the entire trial process has been an extraordinary challenge. It draws on the accumulated wisdom I have received over the years from lawyers, clients, judges, and juries. To single out a few individuals guarantees that I will miss others. However, with apologies and thanks to those I miss, I want to give special thanks to some of the people who made this book possible.

This book is the second edition of *Going to Trial*, first published by the American Bar Association in 1989. I owe a debt of gratitude to all those who contributed to the first edition:

Karl Beckmeyer	Tavernier, Florida
Marjorie Crowder Briggs	Columbus, Ohio
Stephen C. Buser	Columbia, Illinois
R. Carl Cannon	Atlanta, Georgia
G. Ware Cornell, Jr.	Fort Lauderdale, Florida
Cameron C. Gamble	New Orleans, Louisiana
Stephen Kelly	Phoenix, Arizona
Kevin M. Myles	Lake Forest, Illinois
William J. O'Connor II	Billings, Montana
Dennis L. Peterson	Minneapolis, Minnesota
John T. Phipps	Champaign, Illinois
Jill A. Smith	Columbus, Ohio
Robert A. Woodke	Bemidji, Minnesota

I am equally indebted to the following for their contributions to the second edition:

- Neil Aresty, President of Legal Computer Solutions, Inc. (www.lcsweb.com), who has mastered the interrelationship between litigation and technology and generously shared it with the rest of us in Chapter 3.
- My law partners, Tom Butters and John Brazilian, and everyone at Butters, Brazilian & Small, L.L.P., for their patience and advice.

Particular thanks to Sarah Corrigan, Meaghan Barrett, and my assistant Suzanne Mullen for their assistance above and beyond the call of duty.
- Jane Johnston and everyone on the ABA staff.
- Eunice Clavner and the General Practice Section Publications Board for their faith and support.
- Several great friends and great trial lawyers who gave of their time and experience, including Stephen Lyons and Victor Koufman.
- My wife, Alix, and our children, Bailey, Gabrielle, and Schuyler, for their love, patience, and support.

Introduction to the Second Edition

Trials are how society lawfully settles disputes that cannot be settled by other means. During a trial, lawyers are the advocates for their clients. In that role, they face constant scrutiny from all sides: opposing counsel, the court, the jury, and of course, the client. The pressure and demands can be oppressive, and lawyers need all the help they can get.

This is as it should be. We have come some distance from the ancient trial by combat or trial by fire, but trials are still intense, important events that decide crucial matters. When I teach Trial Advocacy, law students and young lawyers often ask, "How or when do I stop being nervous?" My response is always the same: The day you are not nervous walking into court is the day you should quit and do something else. Trials are too important and demanding for anyone not to be nervous. They require a level of focus and alertness that is not compatible with calmness.

How, then, do we help lawyers get ready for trial? It has often been said that the three most important rules for going to trial are preparation, preparation, and preparation. Trials are full of surprises, but we can minimize them by careful planning. This book is intended to provide the general practitioner with a single volume reference to the basic steps, techniques, and points to consider in preparing and trying a case. It is not meant to be a definitive analysis of trial procedure. As such, it has been a daunting, and somewhat presumptuous, effort. Any of the chapters, and often any section of a chapter, could be the subject of a separate book. Indeed, we have included some of these titles in the recommended "Further Reading" section.

The outlines, checklists, and forms provided in this book are meant to be illustrative only and do not purport to cover all situations or legal requirements in all cases or jurisdictions. The reader is expected to determine the particular procedural and substantive requirements of any case he or she may handle for a client in their particular jurisdiction.

I will admit to my prejudices. I love trials. After almost twenty years as a trial lawyer, I believe that trials are among the greatest professional challenges lawyers face and the most extraordinary drama anywhere. A large part of the challenge is understanding, becoming comfortable with, and preparing for each step. There is no magic to achieving this goal, just experience and hard work. This book is intended to help make the basics of that process easier to master, so you can concentrate more on your particular case and client. Use it in that spirit, and good luck in court!

Daniel I. Small

Forms in Chapter 1

1 | Initial Interview and Opening the File

Time and again, busy lawyers get to trial and bemoan the fact that they are not organized, can't find anything, and didn't have time to prepare. They usually fail to recognize two critical points. First, the key to organization and preparation is to start at the beginning, from the moment the client walks in the door. A little time spent up front can eliminate a great deal of time, trouble, and embarrassment at trial. Second, much of what needs to be done to organize a case can be anticipated and simplified through good systems and the use of standard forms.

The actual handling of a case most often begins with the initial interview. It provides the lawyer with the opportunity to collect the information necessary to evaluate the client and the case, provides the foundation for proper case organization, and sets the ground rules for the relationship between lawyer and client. Such a critical step should involve careful consideration, preparation, execution, and follow-up.

I. Interview Goals

1. Establish rapport with client, explain the attorney-client relationship and privilege, and identify the client's goals for litigation.
2. Obtain basic information about the litigation event and damages and decide what other information you need for your evaluation.
3. Learn about the client.
   a. Is the client able to afford litigation emotionally and financially?
   b. Is the client personally compatible with you?

4. Consider possible theories about the litigation event and develop a factual investigation and case plan.

5. Explain to your client in a general way what the possible outcomes are and what to expect during the progress of the case.

6. Discuss the cost of litigation and agree on fees.

II. Preparation for Initial Interview

When you make the appointment, ask your client to bring all pertinent documents and evidence, such as contracts, policies, reports, bills, and photographs, to the initial interview. Depending on the person and situation, you may also want to ask the client to write a full account of the matter in a memo to you (to preserve confidentiality). In some cases, the written account can wait until after the initial interview, but in any event always reassure your client that it is only a draft, and you will surely come up with more details by working together. If possible and appropriate, your client may bring friendly witnesses to be interviewed at the same time.

Depending on the case, you may want to do a little research to prepare for the initial interview. For example, look in local newspapers and the Internet for information on individuals or entities involved. Read or talk to people about the particular industry or field pertinent to the events. Pull and review some cases with similar fact patterns or legal issues. Finally, try to schedule the interview so that you have a period of uninterrupted time. A solid block of time will allow you to focus on the new case, as well as give your client comfort that you are taking his or her situation seriously.

III. Manner and Method of Interview

Imagine sitting on a park bench next to a total stranger and asking him probing and embarrassing personal questions. He would think you were crazy. You should no more expect a client to come to you (usually a stranger) and immediately and openly tell you everything about his or her life and litigation. You cannot properly represent your client unless you know the facts, but getting them requires patience, persistence, and compassion.

In an initial interview, you should control the conversation, but after some introductory comments, let the client talk first: about herself, her background, and why she has consulted you. Allow her to tell her story for awhile before you begin to clarify specific facts. Above all, be a good listener.

Once you begin to focus on the facts, you need to do so in as complete and organized fashion as possible.

1. Develop a written chronology of the events.
2. Develop a plan to offer evidence (testimonial or documentary) to prove each element of your case.
3. Tie in client's documents with chronology.
4. Continually ask your client for anything else she may have recalled during questions.

In obtaining basic information, it helps to use standardized interview questionnaires or checklists. (For example, see Personal Injury Questionnaires, Forms 1–8 and 1–9.) Initial questionnaires may be partially or completely filled out by the client, with or without a legal assistant, before seeing you. However, completing the forms independently adds an element of impersonality and may be inappropriate under some circumstances.

Clients rarely tell lawyers everything in an initial interview. Multiple interviews may be required, particularly if the case is complex or if your client is uncomfortable. Subsequent interviews are also helpful to ensure that your client's position and goals have not changed over the course of long litigation.

While the client is in your office, obtain all pertinent documents and give him or her a list of all other materials to gather in order to assist in the investigation or preparation of the case. Have the client sign all appropriate authorizations so that you can obtain medical, police, military, employment and wage loss, or other records.

IV. Fee Discussion and Agreements

Your fee should be discussed and clearly agreed to at your initial conference. The complete terms should be put in writing and signed by your client or confirmed by a letter to the client. Sample Agreements are enclosed as Form 1–4, General Retainer/Hourly Billing Agreement, and Form 1–5, Contingent Fee Agreement. Make sure your client understands that *you have not been retained* until both of you have signed the fee agreement and paid any retainer. Do not accept suit papers or agree to enter any appearance until you have been retained, the fee agreement signed, and your retainer paid; be sure to advise the client of any response deadlines.

Some jurisdictions regulate to some extent the type of fee that may be charged (contingent fees, and so forth) or have specific requirements for the content of written fee agreements (for example, retainer agreements). Be sure you are familiar with these ethical and statutory requirements and that you have fully explained them to your client at the outset to avoid misunderstandings.

V. Evaluating and Rejecting Cases

Evaluate both the client and the case carefully. Problem cases and problem clients often carry red warning flags. Problem clients can include the following characteristics or behaviors.

1. Client has had prior lawyer who was fired or withdrew.
2. Client has personality or character defects (untrustworthy, deceptive, unsympathetic, and so on).
3. Client has suspect motives for litigation (for example, greed, harassment, revenge, or retribution).
4. Client has unrealistic expectations (immediate results, impossible deadlines, larger recovery, or greater remedies than possible or probable).
5. Client is too emotionally involved given what is at issue.
6. Client believes there is no way he or she can lose.

Even the best or most appealing or sympathetic client can come in with a problem case, such as the following:

1. Statute of limitations period has or is about to expire.
2. Case does not make economic sense: likely minimal damages, time required and costs of proof are high.
3. There is no realistic probability that you can save the client or improve his position.
4. The suit would draw counterclaims, particularly in cases you would handle on a contingency basis.
5. The case involves issues outside your areas of expertise, experience, or interest.

If you doubt the merits of the case, the veracity of the client, his or her ability to pay your fees, or your compatibility, trust your instincts and reject the case. Moreover, put the rejection in writing (see Form 1–3, Case Declination Letter).

VI. Explanation of Litigation Process

With all the other pressures on their time, lawyers often forget that even sophisticated clients do not know some of the most basic elements of litigation. That litigation is unpredictable certainly should be explained to the client. However, unpredictability is no excuse not to describe thoroughly what may lie ahead. Explain the steps of litigation, including the complaint, written discovery, depositions, temporary orders, and other pleadings, and events such as independent medical exams that are likely to occur. Discuss the timing, possible delays, and uncertainties in each step and what may be required of the client along the way.

Take the time to fully explain the attorney-client relationship and each of your roles in litigation. Tell your client how you will communicate progress, settlement discussions, and the circumstances under which he or she should contact you such as new evidence, or changes in address, health, employment, or marital status. With that introduction, you should enlist the client's help and participation in preparation of the case by providing him or her with a list of things to do.

1. Prepare (or review and revise, if already started) a memo to you setting forth all the relevant facts.
2. Bring in and secure all documents and physical evidence.
3. Keep a daily diary and other appropriate records.
4. Keep a record of expenses, prescriptions, transportation, and other items of damages, as appropriate.
5. Continue with any medical treatment.
6. Remind the client *not* to discuss the case with others or sign anything without your permission.

If appropriate, give your client a written reminder list of instructions (see Client Questionnaire, Form 1–6).

VII. Opening and Organizing the File

When the client arrives at the office, have him or her complete a client questionnaire form and include all pertinent personal and case information. Make sure that the client signs the retainer agreement and authorization forms for disclosure of information before leaving the office. After you accept the assignment, make sure your secretary or legal assistant creates the file and has the following documents:

1. New Matter Checklist (Form 1–1);
2. New Matter Report (Form 1–2);
3. Signed Retainer Agreement (Form 1–4 or 5);
4. Signed Authorization Forms (Forms 1–9, 10, 11); and
5. Client Questionnaire (fully executed) (Form 1–6).

Every lawyer and every law firm develops its own filing system. The keys are to have an easily understandable and accessible system (for example, alphabetical), with new numbers and files for each matter, all of which tie into a general client/matter list for potential conflict of interest and reference purposes. The New Matter Checklist outlines a fairly extensive system, which you can either adapt for your own use or use to generate ideas and improvements in your existing system.

When a new matter is opened, create a case file *immediately* (even if you have little or nothing to put in it), with likely subfiles. The subfiles should be labeled with the matter name and subject of the file, such as, "Smith: Correspondence" or "SMI-1: Correspondence." There are a number of reasons for organizing your files in this manner.

1. It cuts down on the chance that papers will be lost.
2. It means that you are organized from the beginning and not playing catch-up later on when the file is a mess and you can't find what you need.
3. It allows you to bring parts of a file to court or a meeting without moving the entire file.

The most common subfiles include the following:

Correspondence

All correspondence relating to the case should be tacked down in a file in reverse chronological order (most recent on the top). Everything, including cover letters, letters sent and received, fax confirmation sheets, hard copies of e-mail, and so forth should be kept in Correspondence. If documents or other materials come with a cover letter, and you want to keep the cover letter with these materials in a separate file, put a copy of the cover letter in Correspondence, so your Correspondence file will be complete.

The Correspondence file will become your record of the case. You never know when a dispute will arise in the course of litigation, and you'll need evidence that something was sent or received. You should also consider maintaining a separate office-wide chronological file as a backup for all correspondence sent out for all matters.

Pleadings

As pleadings are served or filed, they should be tacked down in reverse chronological order, tabbed, and indexed. Where a pleading is too large for the file, make an entry for it in the index anyway and reference the fact that it is in a separate file. With discovery, it is a good practice to number the documents you produce and to keep a clean copy of your production in the file (if you need to use a document, make a working copy).

Medical Records (two options for filing)

a) If you are anticipating a lot of records, keep a medical record file *and* a medical bill file for each provider. (Note: when you are requesting medical records, many providers now have separate record and billing departments; therefore, one request will not always produce all of the client's records and bills. A separate request, with an authorization from the client, should be sent to each department).

b) If you are *not* anticipating a lot of records, keep a file for the records obtained from each provider, or keep files for all records obtained and a separate file for the bills. (Note: when you request medical records, always request a certified copy—that way, you won't have to go back and have them certified prior to trial in order to use them as exhibits).

Liens

In a personal injury case, you should keep all of the liens placed on the case in a separate file.

Notes/Memos

It is a good idea to keep a file for your notes or internal memos. It is an even better idea to make and keep a quick note regarding each telephone conversation or meeting you have regarding the case. Anything you can do to make a record of the way you handled the case or to document events in the case can help you down the line.

Research

Depending on the complexity of the case, you can either keep all your research in one file marked "Smith: Research" or in separate files by issue, "Smith/Research/Limitations."

Expenses/Billing

Especially in a contingent fee case, it is a good idea to keep a file for your expenses. These would include receipts for copies of medical records, a receipt for the filing fee if the case is put into suit, and so forth. As with the Lien file, it will make your life easier when it comes time to disburse the settlement. In a normal billing case, keep copies of bills in the file for reference.

VIII. The Docket System

Trial lawyers live or die by the calendar. There are many ways to keep track of key dates, but whatever method you use, make sure that you have a system that everyone clearly understands and rigorously follows, that the person responsible for entering and circulating dates is identified, and that an effective backup system exists. Important dates should be entered as soon as they are known, not at some unspecified later time. These dates may include the following:

1. all statute of limitations dates;
2. all procedural deadlines (responsive pleadings, and so forth);
3. all required appearances, including dates for trials, hearings, and depositions;
4. all dates for current matters, including interrogatories, document preparation, research, and commitments to clients;
5. all appointments and dates for follow-up calls or letters.

Elements in Docket-Control System

The docket control system should include several elements. First, a perpetual calendar, either on paper (index cards) or computer. An example is described in detail in section 6.07 of *A Practical Guide to Preventing Legal Malpractice* by Stern and Felix-Retzke (Shepard's McGraw-Hill, 1983). Second, a tickler file, for reminder and reference. Third, an appointment calendar, located at or accessible from your and your secretary's desk. Computer appointment calendars can work wonders.

Responsibility for Maintaining System

Normally, the secretary makes all entries into the docket control system. The lawyer and the paralegal, however, are responsible for informing the secretary of all dates and events that should be placed in the system and periodically reviewing the entries of others. When the client's file is opened, the lawyer fills out the New Matter Report and enters the statute of limitation date in the space provided. In addition, either the lawyer or the paralegal may complete the New Matter Checklist and insert not only the actual date of an event or deadline, but also:

1. with respect to the statute of limitations, dates 7, 30, and/or 60 days prior to the date or event;
2. with respect to court dates, a date 7 days prior to the appearance;
3. with respect to deadlines imposed by written agreement of parties to the transaction, dates 7 and/or 14 days prior.

IX. Staffing the Case

For any lawyer, deciding how to staff a case—how many people, at what level, who, and when—can involve difficult decisions and juggling of resources. For the solo practitioner or small firm lawyer, those challenges can be particularly significant. The temptation to under-staff a case and just "do the best you can" can be great but should be strongly resisted. The bottom line is: (1) do not take a case you cannot handle; and (2) very few cases should be handled entirely by one person. The good news is that help is available if you are determined and creative.

Secretary

Many lawyers stubbornly fail to acknowledge just how important the secretary or assistant is to trial organization and preparation. In addition to the standard word processing and document preparation, a competent legal secretary can perform a number of other litigation tasks, including:

- maintaining and updating the files. Piles of unfiled documents are an invitation to disaster. Keeping up with the case filing and file management is essential.
- maintaining and updating the core documents. Once a system is developed, this can be a relatively straightforward and incredibly useful function.
- calendaring and tickler lists.
- time entry and billing. Whether your case is on an hourly rate or contingent fee basis, don't forget to keep track of your time carefully and bill regularly as appropriate (even if the bill is only internal). It is easy to get behind and hard to catch up.
- other tasks. Sit down with your secretary or assistant and decide what other tasks he or she can and should handle. Learn to delegate and supervise effectively.

Law Clerk

In many areas, there are law schools filled with students who would love to get involved in a real trial. Get a clear time commitment: both a daily or weekly schedule and a duration (one month, six months). Then assign tasks, possibly including:

- legal research, jury instructions;
- reviewing or summarizing documents or transcripts, as appropriate;
- assisting in other tasks (witness interviews, and so forth).

Paralegal

Many law firms are top-heavy: too many lawyers and not enough support staff. The result is that either lawyers do tasks that a paralegal or other staff member could do as well (or better) or important case organization tasks are simply not being done, or both. If you do not have, or cannot support, sufficient paralegal help, there are lots of options for part-time or temporary staffing. As you go through this book, many of the forms that are key to developing and organizing your case can and should be done—at least in the first instance—by a paralegal or other nonlawyers. Think about what your needs are as you read.

Lawyer

How much motion practice, how many documents, how many depositions (when, where), how long and difficult is trial, and how many opposing lawyers will there be trying to overwhelm you? Do you need one or more junior lawyers, another more senior lawyer? Then, where do you find the right people: within your firm, from friends or other firms, either by barter or independent contracting, temporary agencies for lawyers, or some other method? There are lots of opportunities for flexible staffing these days, so base your judgment on what you *need* to properly staff the case first, and *then* worry about how to get it.

Now the file is open, the client has been interviewed, the case organized and staffed, and the real work of litigation begins. Without this solid organizational foundation, your subsequent work on the case can be as unstable as a house of cards, ready to fall on you at any point. Begin on the right foot, and you will benefit from your early efforts as you proceed with the case.

Further Reading

Baurn, David. *Art of Advocacy—Preparation of a Case*. Albany, NY: Matthew Bender, 1981.

Fortas, Abe. "The Legal Interview." *Psychiatry* 15 (February 1952): 91.

Hartje, Jeffrey H. and Mark E. Wilson, *Lawyer's Work*, Seattle, WA, Butterworth Legal Publishers, 1984.

Hurowitz. "How to Handle a New Client, Preparation for the Initial Meeting." *Practical Lawyer* 21 (1975): 11.

The Lawyer's Handbook, ICLE. Hutchins Hall, Ann Arbor, Mich. 48109.

Ross, J.H. "The Initial Interview." *Psychoanalysis* 5 (1957): 46–57.

Royal, Robert F. and Steve R. Schutt. *The Gentle Art of Interviewing and Interrogation*. Englewood Cliffs, NJ: Prentice-Hall, 1976.

Watson, Andrews. *The Lawyer in the Interviewing and Counseling Process*. Indianapolis, Ind.: Bobbs-Merrill, 1976.

1-1. NEW MATTER CHECKLIST

Date: _____

Re: _____

Code: _____

	Do	**Done**	(date)

1. __ _____ Prepare new matter report

2. __ _____ Give lawyer checklist for following area of law: _____

3. __ _____ Assign file number (consult file number notebook)

4. __ _____ Enter file number in file number notebook and on new matter report

5. __ _____ Place copy of new matter report in notebook and distribute

6. __ _____ Prepare fee agreement: _____

7. __ _____ Prepare letter to client re: retainer and fee agreement

8. __ _____ Stamp file when retainer is paid and signed agreement form is returned

9. __ _____ Prepare reminder/assignment cards/notations for following items

			Actual Date	Advance Reminder Date(s)
__	_____	Statute of limitations:	_____	_____
__	_____	Court date:	_____	_____
__	_____	Other (namely):	_____	_____

10. __ _____ Prepare client account sheet (ledger sheet) and place in file

11. __ _____ Prepare file and subfile manila folders, organize file

12. __ _____ Place this checklist in one-week follow-up file and case subfile

1-2. NEW MATTER REPORT

Case Code: _____

Client: _____ Date _____ 19/20_____

Address: _____ New Client __ Present Client____

City:_____ State:___ Zip: _____ Soc. Sec. # _____

Business Phone: _____ FAX: _____

Contact: _____ Home Phone: _____

File Name: _____

Nature of Matter: _____

_____

Amount Involved: _____ Area of Practice Code: _____

Opposing Party: _____

Opposing Party: _____

Referred by: _____

__ Fixed Fee of $ _____

__ Time Rate: _____ Retainer: _____

__ Contingency of: _____

__ Other _____

Billing Instructions: _____

_____

Statute of Limitations:

Originating Lawyer:

Supervising Lawyer:

Associate Assigned:

1-3. CASE DECLINATION LETTER

Dear _____,

    It was a pleasure to meet you on _____, 19/20___, and to have the opportunity to discuss_____. I certainly sympathize with what you have been through. However, as we discussed, after review and consideration, I am declining professional responsibility for the matter. {optional: The reason for declining the case is that _____.}

    For your information, based on what you have told me, I believe that the statute of limitations or other relevant time period on any claim you may have in this regard may expire as early as _____. You may have to act prior to that time if you wish to protect the claim. {Note: Use the most restrictive statute, for example, the earliest statute of limitations date.}

    Another lawyer may reach a different conclusion or may wish to take the case, but you should seek additional counsel before the deadline expires. Again, thank you for the opportunity to meet with you on this matter.

Best Wishes,

_____

{cc: Referring Lawyer}

1-4. GENERAL RETAINER/HOURLY BILLING AGREEMENT

DATED this____day of _____, 19/20__, the undersigned client(s) retains and employs _____ as his/her/their lawyer to represent him/her/them relating to: _____

The undersigned agree(s) to pay as attorney's fees the following:

(a) _____ as and for a retainer; and

(b) _____ per hour for partner, _____ per hour for associate, and _____ per hour for paralegal or legal assistant services expended on behalf of undersigned, with billing on a monthly basis, due within 30 days.

The undersigned understands that the lawyer is not retained and will not commence work until this agreement is signed and the retainer is paid in full. The undersigned further agrees that, in addition to the above lawyer's fees, all costs, including court costs, subpoena costs, photographs, depositions, court reporter costs, reports, witness statements, and all other out-of-pocket expenses directly incurred in investigating or litigating this claim shall be billed monthly and paid by the undersigned.

1. This contract shall be governed by the law of the state of_____.
2. The undersigned covenants and agrees to pay and discharge all reasonable costs, lawyer's fees, and expenses that shall be incurred and made by the lawyer in enforcing the terms of this agreement.
3. On accounts outstanding over 30 days, the undersigned covenants and agrees to pay to lawyer interest on the average daily balance at the highest rate allowable by law, or 18 percent, if no such amount is set by law.
4. On accounts outstanding over 60 days, all work by the lawyer and staff shall cease until the account is paid in full or a payment plan is agreed upon.
5. If the undersigned is not completely truthful with lawyer or unreasonably fails to follow lawyer's advice, undersigned agrees that lawyer may withdraw as counsel.
6. Lawyer makes no representation as to the cost, likely resolution or possible outcome of this or any matter.

THE UNDERSIGNED HAS RECEIVED A COPY OF THIS CONTRACT.

_____ (Client)(Seal) _____(Witness)

by: _____

_____ (Lawyer)(Seal) _____(Witness)

1-5. CONTINGENT FEE AGREEMENT

DATED this _____ day of _____, 19/20__, the undersigned client(s) retains and employs _____ as my/our lawyer to represent me/us with full authorization and to do all things necessary to prosecute all my/our claims arising from or relating to _____

My/our lawyer agrees to undertake the investigation and preparation of these claims and the prosecution of appropriate actions to recover damages due as a result of such claims. No promises have been made as to the probability of recovery. I/we agree to cooperate with my/our lawyer as requested in locating documents and witnesses, securing testimony, preparing for legal proceedings, and in other matters as desired by him/her.

The attorney's fee shall be _____ percent of any and all monies recovered or obtained, including by settlement or judgment, relating in any way to these claims. If I/we do not cooperate in the litigation or if I/we discharge my/our lawyer, I/we agree to pay him/her a fee computed on a time expended basis at rates of ____per hour for partner, _____ per hour for associates, and _____ per hour for paralegals and assistants.

I/we realize it will be necessary for my/our lawyer to advance certain expenses during the course of litigation, and I/we agree to reimburse him/her for all expenses advanced. Those expenses shall be subtracted from any sum recovered after the attorney fee is deducted. In the event no recovery is made, I/we are still responsible for payment of the expenses. However, if no recovery is made, I/we will not be responsible for any attorney fee.

I/we understand that no settlement shall be made without my/our consent. I/we have received a copy of this contract as well as a copy of the applicable Rules of Professional Responsibility.

We have each carefully read and fully understand the above agreement.

_____ (Client)(Seal) _____(Witness)

_____ (Client)(Seal) _____(Witness)

_____ (Lawyer)(Seal) _____(Witness)

1-6. CLIENT QUESTIONNAIRE

Date of Interview: File No.:
Referred by: Court No.:

Client Name: _____ Age: _____

Address: _____ County: _____

Home Phone: _____ Soc. Sec. No.: _____

Employer: _____

Address: _____

Business Phone: _____ FAX/E-mail: _____

Checklist of Discussions:

   Assignments to client:

      ___Factual memos: _____
      ___Books and financial records: _____
      ___Papers and contracts: _____
      ___Documents regarding damages: _____
      ___Income tax returns: _____
      ___Other items (please list): _____
      _____
      _____
      _____

   Discussions:

      ___ Court procedures explained
      ___ Office procedures explained
      ___ Fees agreed to
      ___ Summary of facts completed

Provided to Client:

      ___Copy of Retention/Fee Agreement
      ___Witness Briefing Memo
      ___Other: _____

1-7. PERSONAL INJURY CHECKLIST

Re:

File Number:_____ Date of Loss:_____

Do	Date Required	Date Received	_____ Item of Work_____
—	_____	_____	1. Client executed retainer agreement
—	_____	_____	2. Client executed authorization forms
—	_____	_____	3. Police/fire report
—	_____	_____	4. Photographs
—	_____	_____	5. Police interview
—	_____	_____	6. Dispose of traffic citation against client
—	_____	_____	7. Motor vehicle report (Form SR–1 for Illinois)
—	_____	_____	8. Letters to witnesses
—	_____	_____	9. Witness statements
—	_____	_____	10. Damage estimate of personal property
—	_____	_____	11. Wage verification
—	_____	_____	12. Medical records
—	_____	_____	13. Medical bills
—	_____	_____	14. Doctor's reports
—	_____	_____	15. Doctor's office notes
—	_____	_____	16. Hospital report/nurse's minutes
—	_____	_____	17. Other proofs of loss
—	_____	_____	18. Demand for appraisal
—	_____	_____	19. Letter to insurance company with documentation of injuries or claims
—	_____	_____	20. Demand letter for settlement
—	_____	_____	21. Complaint and summons
—	_____	_____	22. Answer
—	_____	_____	23. Interrogatories
—	_____	_____	24. Request to produce document, and so on
—	_____	_____	25. Answers to interrogatories
—	_____	_____	26. Request to disclose expert
—	_____	_____	27. Depositions (list names of subjects)
—	_____	_____
—	_____	_____
—	_____	_____

1-8. PERSONAL INJURY: AUTOMOBILE INTERVIEW SHEET

Referred by: _____

Date: _____

Name: _____ Age: _____

Address: _____ Home Phone: _____

Marital Status: _____ Name of Spouse/Parent: _____

Employer:_____

Job Description: _____

Address: _____

Weekly or Yearly Gross Income: _____

Passenger: _____ Driver: _____

Previous Injury History:

(1) _____

_____

(2) _____

_____

Did client make a statement to anyone other than this office? Details:

(1) _____

_____

(2) _____

_____

Does client carry medical insurance?

Amount: _____ Company: _____

Automobile Insurance:

_____ Company: _____

Uninsured Motorists' Insurance:

_____ Company: _____

Client's Vehicle: _____ Year: _____

Type of vehicle: _____

Owner of vehicle: _____

Driven from accident scene: _____ Towed by whom: _____

Approximate damage to vehicle: _____

Client advised to obtain two (2) estimates: _____

Client advised to photograph damage: _____
Accident:
Date: _____ Time: _____ Location: _____

Description:

Names and addresses of persons who will have knowledge of client's case:

    Witnesses: _____
    _____

    Work related: _____
    _____

    Family: _____
    _____

    Friends: _____
    _____

Are Photographs Advisable: (car, scar, intersection, cast, and so forth) _____
Are photographs ordered: _____

Is investigation indicated: _____
Name of investigator: _____ Phone: _____ Ordered: _____
Was there any drinking involved: _____
Were police notified: _____ Was police report made: _____
City: _____ County: _____ State highway: ____ Other: _____

Were Any Arrests Made:_____ **Disposition of Hearing if Known:**_____

Defendants:
    Name: _____
    Address: _____ State License: _____
    Name: _____
    Address: _____ State License: _____
    Name of defendant's insurance carrier or broker: _____

Medical:
    Attending doctor: _____ Address: _____
    Other doctors (first aid, consultants, etc.): _____
    _____ Address: _____

Nature of injuries: _____
Hospital: _____

Damages:

     Property damage: $_____ Documents: _____

     Medical bills: _____ Documents: _____

     Lost time, etc.: _____ Documents: _____

     Other: _____ Documents: _____

Has Client Been Instructed:

     1. To give no information to anyone other than our office?_____

     2. To be patient?_____

     3. To forward to this office all bills or receipts for damages?_____

1-9. PERSONAL INJURY WITNESS REPORT
FORM: MOTOR VEHICLE ACCIDENT

Name of Client: Current Date: _____

File No.:   Date of Accident: _____

1. Name: 2. Date of Birth:

3. Home Address/Phone Number:

4. Business Address/Phone Number:

5. Occupation/Position:

6. Name/address/phone of person who will always know how to contact you.

7. What, if any, is your relationship to the parties to this accident?

8. Recollection of accident:

    a.   When did it happen—time and date?

    b.   Where did it occur?

    c.   What were you doing? Where were you coming from/going?

    d.   Please describe the motor vehicles involved in the accident (make/model/year/operating condition/appearance).

    e.   Where were you when the accident occurred?

    f.   Describe everything you saw and heard.
        1) Lighting
        2) Weather conditions
        3) Condition of road or pavement
        4) Accident

    g.   Did anything obstruct your view of the accident?

    h.   Was the accident a result of a particular defect (improper lighting, defective sign, nonfunctioning traffic signals, bumps or holes in pavement)?

9.   Do you have any problem with eyesight? If so, please explain. Do you wear eyeglasses?

10. Did you do anything after the accident? (Did you give statements? Did you talk to any parties or discuss the accident with anybody?) If so, please give details.

11. If you heard any conversations, who said what to whom, and who else was present to hear comments?

12. Did anyone admit fault or responsibility for the accident? If so, describe what was said, where, and who was present.

13. Medical Injuries

   a. Did anyone appear to be injured in any way? If so, describe your impressions.

   b. Was any medical assistance rendered at the scene of the accident?

   c. If so, by whom?

   d. Where was the injured person taken?

14. Since the accident, have you been contacted by anyone to discuss your knowledge of it? If so, please give details.

15. Have you given any statements or signed any reports regarding the accident? If so, please give details.

16. Have you ever testified in any court proceeding before? If so, please give details.

ACKNOWLEDGMENT

I have read the above statement, and it is true and accurate to the best of my knowledge, recollection, and belief.

_____
Witness

Subscribed and sworn to before me on this _____day of ____, 19/20___.

_____
Notary Public

1-10. AUTHORIZATION TO RELEASE MEDICAL AND/OR HOSPITAL RECORDS AND BILLS

To: _____ Address: _____

Patient: _____ Address: _____

    You are hereby authorized to furnish and release to my lawyer, _____, [address, tel. no.] or any of his or her representatives, all medical and billing information and records, including results of examination, tests, diagnoses, records, treatment and prognoses. Further, I hereby authorize you and your representatives to discuss all aspects of any treatment with my lawyer. Please do not disclose information to insurance adjusters or any other persons without written authority from me (pursuant to confidential and privileged communications laws). All prior authorizations are hereby canceled. The foregoing authority shall continue in force until revoked by me in writing, but no longer than one year from the below date. This information is necessary for my lawyer to represent me in regard to my injuries. Thank you for your cooperation.

_____, 19/20___   X_____
                                    Patient (if minor, adult with authority to act;
                                    if patient deccased, legal representative)

_____

Witness

_____

Witness

Please attach your invoice for any copying cost and send with requested records to my
office.

Approximate date(s) service rendered   Thank you,

_____
_____
_____19/20____   _____
                                                Attorney-at-Law

                                                _____

                                                _____

1-11. AUTHORIZATION FOR
WAGE AND SALARY INFORMATION

To: _____

This authorization or photocopy hereof authorizes you to furnish any and all information you may have regarding my wages or salary while I was employed by you to my lawyer _____ [address, tel. no.], or any or his or her representatives. This includes any personal records and any and all information or records concerning wages or other compensation lost in connection with injuries I received in [description of accident] on [date]. I further authorize you to discuss all aspects of my employment and compensation with my lawyer. Thank you for your cooperation.

_____   _____

Signature   Date

Name: _____   Social Security Number: _____

1-12. REQUEST FOR POLICE REPORT

Dated: _____

[Town] Police Department
[Street]
[Town], [State], [Zip]

Dear Sir or Madam:

Kindly furnish my attorney, [Name / Firm /Address] or any of his her representatives, with a copy of any reports and/or photographs prepared in connection with an incident in which I was [description of accident/incident, including date, time and exact location in Town]. Thank you.

_____

[Client]

Name: _____

Address: _____

_____

1-13. CASE STATUS CHECKLIST

Check Action—To Do	Deadline	Completed	Check Action—To Do	Deadline	Completed
___ Insurance coverage	_____	_____	___ Expert's reports	_____	_____
___ D's auto ownership	_____	_____	___ Blowups—document evidence	_____	_____
___ City directory info.	_____	_____	___ X rays and medical illus.	_____	_____
___ Newspaper articles/ photos	_____	_____	___ Models	_____	_____
___ Corporate agents	_____	_____	___ Statement of facts	_____	_____
___ Photos— P's injuries	_____	_____	___ Outline issues and research	_____	_____
___ Photos—scene (aerial?)	_____	_____	___ Analyze pleadings & orders	_____	_____
___ Photos—P's & D's vehicles	_____	_____	___ Amendments to pleadings	_____	_____
___ Motion pictures	_____	_____	___ Outline of proof	_____	_____
___ Statements— witnesses	_____	_____	___ Jury list & investigation	_____	_____
___ Accident reports	_____	_____	___ Opening statement outline	_____	_____
___ Weather reports	_____	_____	___ Witness list & subpoenas	_____	_____
___ Maps & diagrams	_____	_____	___ Direct exam outline	_____	_____
___ Books & records	_____	_____	___ Exhibit index	_____	_____
___ Medical reports	_____	_____	___ Cross-exam outline	_____	_____
___ Hospital records	_____	_____	___ Rebuttal outline	_____	_____
___ Death certificate	_____	_____	___ Jury instruction & authority	_____	_____
___ Coroner's report	_____	_____	___ Trial brief	_____	_____
___ Laboratory reports	_____	_____	___ Expert witness conf.	_____	_____
___ Medical expenses— past/future	_____	_____	___ Lay witness conf.	_____	_____

___ Lost-income   _____ _____   ___ Client conference   _____ _____
verification

___ Property repair   _____ _____   ___ Final argument outline _____ _____
estimates

___ Other special   _____ _____   ___ All witnesses   _____ _____
damages   subpoenaed

Explanation & Instructions (Ref. to Nos. Above)

1.   5.

2.   6.

3.   7.

4.   8.

Estimates

Forms in Chapter 2

2 | Core Documents

Preparation is the key to successful litigation. Organization is the key to preparation. Familiarity is the key to organization. The last link may sound out of place, but it is part of the process. Most people do not make the effort to get organized because they have not developed a system that they are comfortable with. Using organizational skills is not a familiar activity for many people, so they avoid it, much to their later regret.

All of the forms and lists in this book are intended to help you get organized. However, the basic reference tool for trial lawyers is a 3-ring notebook that I call the Trial or Reference Notebook (depending on the nature and status of the matter). There are five essential documents that are the foundation for the entire litigation and should always be in your Trial or Reference Notebook. They are the bedrock on which your case is built, and the process of creating and updating them will help develop your case at every step of the way. I call them the "Core Documents." They are:

1. Case Summary;
2. Cast of Characters and Entities;
3. Chronology;
4. Exhibit List; and
5. Pleadings Index.

The core documents can also help you give your client a better understanding of the case itself and the litigation process. Depending on the nature of the case and the client, you may want to have the client do the first draft of the Case Summary, Chronology, and Cast of Characters. It is often surprisingly productive to have the client review your drafts. Seeing the facts in this format can push them to think about the case more carefully or in a different light. These insights can be the keys to moving forward.

The role these core documents play will vary somewhat depending on a lawyer's practice. For someone with little trial experience, they can be a welcome guide to help you through uncertain terrain. For a trial veteran, they become like old friends, always there to fall back on when you need them. They will help you think through your case, your theories, and your vulnerabilities. They also help limit the damage from the most common threat to litigation: delay. Having to stop and start work on a case over time is much easier if you have a clear base of reference from which to restart. The core documents will give you that base, whether the delay is a week, a month, or a year. They will also help others get up to speed quickly as they help you on the case.

What follows is a brief overview of each document, with sample formats provided as appendixes. Each form is also available on the diskette. You can certainly make your own modifications with experience, but to get started, try to use these models as presented.

I. Case Summary

The process of drafting a one to two page case summary, which includes an actual brief summary of the case and a condensed list of key issues, has three principal goals. The first is to force you to focus on what the case is about in a way that trial lawyers often do not do until much later in the process. The second is to create a document that will be an easy reference for you, or for anyone who examines the file at a later time. The third is to encourage the process of rethinking and rewriting the summary and key issues as the case moves along.

The summary should be just that—a clear, concise summary of the case. Suppose you were trying to give an honest overview of the case to another lawyer or a trusted friend or relative. What would you really say? What is the case really about? Honest means pros and cons: the summary is not an adversarial presentation, but rather a chance to tell whoever reads the file what is going on.

The key issues should try to briefly identify what is really at issue in the case—factually and/or legally. What will a trial of the case revolve around, and how would you describe these issues to someone not involved in the case?

The case summary section of the trial notebook is also a good place to keep copies of key reference documents. Depending on the case, these may include an organization chart, anatomy chart, diagrams, language from key laws or regulations, key exhibits, or any other documents you are likely to want readily at hand. (See Form 2–1.)

II. Cast of Characters and Entities

The cast of characters should be an expansive list of people and entities who may be involved in the case, whether as parties, lawyers, witnesses, or otherwise. It should:

1. Be arranged alphabetically.
2. Include key contact information, such as name, employer, title, address, telephone, and fax. For people important to the case, make sure you have all possible means of 24-hour contact.
3. Include a very brief description of that person's position and role in the case.
4. Identify that person or entity's counsel, if any. (See Form 2–2.)

To be worthwhile, this document needs to be constantly updated as new information comes in. The possible sources can include your client, pleadings, discovery, testimony, documents, or whatever. Rather than just filing these things as they arrive, add a note to your assistant (or yourself) to also use specific pages as items to "Update C of C." With word processing, it is easily done. With practice, it will allow you to have an up-to-date document that can be extraordinarily useful in remembering who is who, and placing people and entities in the proper perspective.

III. Chronology

A good chronology can be your most important and useful document. It should cover all significant events in the case, with the date, description, and the citation or source included. (See Form 2–3.). In preparing and revising the chronology, you should seek input from your client and anyone else working on the case. It is a good way to bring together everyone's input for a thorough review of what happened, and how it can be proved. Each part of the chronology described below deserves your careful attention.

1. Events. Be inclusive at first. You can always eliminate entries later if the document gets too long (or in complex cases do separate, shorter chronology organized by Key Events). Things that appear minor early on may take on more significance later.
2. Date. The level of precision depends on the circumstances. Sometimes on background matters, just the month or even the year is sufficient. In other cases you may want to get *more* precise and add the time of day, for example, when it involves medical treatment.

3. <u>Description</u>. Forget full sentences or grammar. A short, staccato description of the key fact(s) is sufficient. Include enough information to be understood, without making the description too long to be useable.

4. <u>Cites</u>. Clearly set forth the best source *and* cite for each item (with alternative cites, if appropriate). Source means the type of material it came from (Smith letter, James Depo.) Cite means the best locator (Bates No. __, Exhibit __, pg. __). A source that is fresh in your mind today may not come to mind when you need it next time, unless it is spelled out in the chronology.

Once the chronology is written, update it routinely. Keep (or have someone keep) a "Chrono Update" file, so that anyone reviewing documents, transcripts, or other materials can make notes of new events or cites and put them in the file for later updating.

IV. Exhibit List

Organizing your documents can be the key to organizing your case. Reviewing your documents can be the key to understanding your case. Developing and periodically updating an exhibit list can help you with both tasks. Your exhibit list will undoubtedly expand, shrink, and change dramatically, but it is important to begin it early and revise it regularly. The key information on an exhibit list is:

1. <u>Number.</u> Even though some or all of these may change, it is important to number your exhibits from the outset (preferably using stickies or something else easily removable). Numbering helps your organization, but more importantly helps you to consider the order of presentation.

2. <u>Bates Number.</u> The Bates or other discovery numbering should be included for easy reference. Always number documents provided by you in discovery, and make sure documents coming from the other side are numbered, too (or have it done).

3. <u>Description.</u> A brief identifying description generally including the date, nature, author, and subject matter if possible ("8/1/98 letter Smith to Jones re: Offer"). Since this document may be the base for what you eventually give to the court and opposing counsel, keep the descriptions generic, not editorial.

4. <u>Witness.</u> Identify the witness or witnesses through whom this document should be introduced.

(See Form 2–4.)

V. Pleadings Index

The pleadings index is simply a chronological list of what has been filed in the case, with date filed and description, which is usually the caption or some abbreviated version of it (See Form 2–5.). One interesting note is that some sort of pleadings index is actually done in many law offices but then buried deep in a pleadings binder in the file cabinet. In fact, it is an invaluable reference for the case history and should always be included in the Trial or Reference Notebook.

Litigation is not static. The case that walks into your office may go through many stages of development and changes before it goes to a jury. These core documents provide both a constant point of reference and a means of noting and recording those developments. Think of them not just as documents, but as assistants, each one with a particular focus, but all playing key roles in assisting you as you prepare your case.

2-1 CASE SUMMARY

COMMONWEALTH OF MASSACHUSETTS

SUFFOLK, ss.   Trial Court of Massachusetts
                                                         Superior Court Department

JOHN DOE,	)
Plaintiff,	)
	)
	)
v.	) Civil Action No. 98-0448F
	)
JOHN SMITH and JOHN JONES,	)
Defendants.	)

CASE SUMMARY

Plaintiff: _____   Defendant: _____

- Counsel: _____   - Counsel: _____
          _____   _____
          _____   _____

                    Judge / Court: _____
                          Clerk: _____
                                 _____
                                 _____

Summary:

Key Issues:

2-2 CAST OF CHARACTERS AND ENTITIES

COMMONWEALTH OF MASSACHUSETTS

SUFFOLK, ss.   Trial Court of Massachusetts
                                                 Superior Court Department

---

JOHN DOE,)	
Plaintiff,)	
)	
v.)	Civil Action No. 98-0448F
)	
JOHN SMITH and JOHN JONES,)	
Defendants.)	

CAST OF CHARACTERS AND ENTITIES

Name	Description	Counsel
- Add./Tel./Fax	- Position/Role	-Add./Tel./Fax

2-3 CHRONOLOGY

COMMONWEALTH OF MASSACHUSETTS

SUFFOLK, ss.   Trial Court of Massachusetts
                                               Superior Court Department

JOHN DOE,	)
Plaintiff,	)
	)
v.	) Civil Action No. 98-0448F
	)
JOHN SMITH and JOHN JONES,	)
Defendants.	)

CHRONOLOGY

Date	Description	Cites
8/1/98	Smith offer letter to Jones	Bates No. 258
8/5/98	Jones meeting with Sales Director	Smith Depo., p. 97
8/10/98	Jones Counter Offer	Exhibit 35

2-4 EXHIBIT LIST

Number	Bates	Description	Witness

2-5 PLEADINGS INDEX

COMMONWEALTH OF MASSACHUSETTS

SUFFOLK, ss.   Trial Court of Massachusetts
                                                  Superior Court Department

_____

JOHN DOE,	)	
Plaintiff,	)	
	)	
	)	
v.	)	Civil Action No. 98-0448F
	)	
JOHN SMITH and JOHN JONES,	)	
Defendants.	)	

PLEADINGS INDEX

Tab #	Description	Date Filed
1.	Complaint	5/3/98
2.	Civil Action Cover Sheet	5/3/98
3.	Summons: Smith	5/4/98
4.	Summons: Jones	5/4/98
5.	Return of Service: Smith	5/6/98
6.	Return of Service: Jones	5/7/98
7.	Plaintiff's First Set of Interrogatories to be Answered by Defendant Smith	5/7/98
8.	Plaintiff's First Request for Production of Documents by Defendant Jones	5/7/98
9.	Plaintiff's First Set of Interrogatories to be Answered by Defendant Smith	5/7/98

3 | Technology in Trial Practice

with Neil Aresty, President
Legal Computer Solutions, Inc.

I. Introduction

The importance of technology in preparing a case for trial cannot be underestimated. Computers play an increasingly important role in all aspects of the life of a case: from the initial case evaluation and investigation, to pleading, document preparation and the organizing of the case file, to the presentation of evidence at trial. In fact, some courts have started experimenting with electronic case filing and the submission of briefs in electronic format.

In 1996 the Federal Rules of Procedure (Fed. R. App. P.25, Fed. R. Civ. P. 5, and Fed. R. Bankr. P. 5005) were amended to permit electronic filing in appellate, district and bankruptcy courts under certain circumstances. The amendments permit the federal courts to establish local rules to allow documents to be filed, signed, or verified by *electronic means*. By the time you read this, you should be checking the local rules of your court.

If used correctly, technology can be the great equalizer in any legal battle. It should only take a relatively small investment in personal computer hardware and software to have the tools necessary to deal with all aspects of preparing a case for trial.

This chapter will review the various categories of software applications that the practitioner should consider using in his or her practice in order to effectively manage any case or case load. Given the speed at which technology changes, it is a daunting task to write recommendations in a book format. Toward that end, the chapter will include hypertext link references (that you can type into an Internet web browser) and point to some documents on the Internet which are updated from time to time.

II. Hardware

Any discussion of technology for the law office would have to start with hardware. This area is changing fast. The good news is that over time, prices continue to go down as the amount of computing power and storage go up. As this is written, a standard PC clone, running at state of the art speed, with sufficient RAM and hard disk memory, can be purchased for under $1,000. If you were purchasing a desktop PC today (or even a laptop, which, as a trial lawyer, would be my preference because of its mobility) it should have the following minimal configuration.

- Pentium processor running at 300 mega hertz (Mhz) or higher (500 Mhz is becoming standard)
- 64 mega bytes (MB) or more of random access memory (RAM)
- 8 gigabytes (GB) or more of hard disk space (HD)
- 12x CD-ROM or DVD/CD-ROM drive
- Video graphics card with 4 MB of memory
- 17-inch color monitor
- 56K speed modem and/or network interface card (NIC)
- keyboard and mouse

Hardware is a commodity item today. It is beyond the scope of this chapter to get into a detailed discussion of the variety of components and types of PCs available for your practice. However, if you can get onto the Internet with a web browser, go to www.lcsweb.com/hardware for a listing of computer companies and on line catalogs which contain current hardware configurations and prices. Another good place to look up hardware information is at your local magazine stand. There are many magazines devoted to the subject, and they all list web sites and the most current prices.

III. The Network

In addition to the basic configuration listed above, a word should be said here about networks. We are now in the era of the networked PC. Even if you think you are a solo practitioner and your PC is not connected to a local area (or "office") network, there is no reason for you not to be connected to the Internet. With access to the Internet, you have access to the world's best information resource.

Almost any PC can connect to the Internet through a modem and a subscription service to an Internet Service Provider (ISP). If you do not know how to find a local ISP, just look at the advertisement in the business section of your local newspaper. Or, ask your friends, colleagues, kids, or neighbors. You should be able to get an account to the Internet for as little as $10 to $20 per month. This subscription service should give you an e-mail address (account) so that you can also send and retrieve e-mail and file attachments (for example, work product documents, transcripts, and even current updates to your software).

Proper case preparation requires the exchange of information. Access to the Internet will increasingly become the avenue by which you not only look for fact and legal materials, but also the channel by which you efficiently and securely communicate with clients, witnesses, opposing counsel, and even the courts. See the web sites of bar associations such as the ABA (www.abanet.org) or ATLA (www.atla.org) for examples of information and document exchange, as well as for useful links to other web based sites for lawyers.

IV. Software

"Garbage In, Garbage Out" (GIGO)

Your software applications are only as good as the data (information) that you put into them. There is a natural tendency to think that the power of a computer application is in its "bells and whistles" or the features and functions it has. In fact, you could have the most powerful knowledge management and document assembly system, but it will not do you any good unless your forms, work product, research, and correspondence have been saved and abstracted into the application. The same is true for case management, contact management, conflict of interest, litigation support, or virtually any software. They are only as good as the data that you put in.

One example from the area of litigation support illustrates the point. Millions of dollars are spent every year on the building of document databases, which are really bibliographic abstracts of the documents culled for evidentiary purposes in prosecuting or defending litigation. The process of abstracting (or "coding") the documents is usually done by paralegals or litigation support specialists. When it comes time to prepare for trial, the lawyers are often frustrated by the inability to quickly find and retrieve meaningful information. Why?

First of all, trial lawyers are like the proverbial woodsmen who are too busy chopping down trees to sharpen their axes. Often, they are not involved at the beginning of the process where one had to think about the database structure in the context of the particular litigation. Usually they have little input into designing or understanding the document abstract. As a result, the document database does not contain the pieces of information that they use or think about when referring to evidence. The language used to code a document type is different from the language used by the lawyer or client in referring to the issues of law or fact.

Second, trial lawyers often have little to do with the document abstracting process. Not that they need to be doing the abstracting or coding, but they should be involved early on in the database review. It is only through the meaningful involvement in the building of the database that the litigation support system becomes useful to the trial lawyer. It is a wonder that people spend so much money on litigation support and never see the real benefit. Get involved early, and bring your knowledge, experience, and personal preferences into the process. The investment of time will be richly rewarded.

Case Management

It helps to look at legal matters as a life cycle. In the beginning, you must decide whether or not you are going to handle the matter. If you do take it on, there should be a standard intake procedure whereby you gather basic client and case information, check for conflicts, open a file, docket key dates (for example, statute of limitations), draft fee agreements, and assign a series of tasks in order to start the case rolling.

The aim of case management software has typically been to automate those tasks in one fashion or another. It should also help you organize and better manage the activities, dates, resources, and documents associated with the case. Historically, case/matter management systems evolved out of specific practice areas. There were systems designed for personal injury, bankruptcy, collection, and divorce practices, to name a few. It is important to know what kind of case management needs your practice has before you buy a particular application.

At a minimum, a case/matter management system ought to help the practitioner organize their practice by collecting appointments, deadlines, and other events through a case calendar; keep an online "rolodex" of people they deal with; help manage the case documents and files; and provide a search and reporting mechanism by which you can easily find and list matter information.

All of this can be accomplished with the generic software tools that come inside the standard "office suites," for example, Microsoft Office, Corel WordPerfect Office, or IBM/Lotus Suite. However, building your own case management system will require patience and a deep understanding of the software. For most practitioners this will not be worthwhile. They simply do not have the skills or time.

Take a good look at your practice needs, and then look at the popular case management systems on the market today. The ABA's Law Practice Management section publishes a compendium, comparing some 30 case management programs, *Computerized Case Management Systems,* by Andrew Z. Adkins, III, http://www.abanet.org/lpm/catalog/511-0409.html.

Amicus Attorney by Gavel & Gown (www.amicus.ca) is an example of a popular generic case management system. It is customizable for different types of practices and integrates with other third party products in order to offer more powerful time and billing and document assembly. It becomes the central launch pad for everything you do in your practice.

TimeMatters by the Data.TXT (www.timematters.com) is another popular application. TimeMatters does not take over the desktop interface the way Amicus does. It works with a more table oriented database structure and may be more customizable than Amicus Attorney. If you want either of these systems to perform at the highest level of functionality, recognizing and hyperlinking to e-mail and web sites, pointing and clicking on documents referenced inside the database tables in order to launch the underlying application, then you should be using the 32 bit version. Both applications sell a 16 bit (optimized for Windows 3.0 and 3.1) and a 32 bit (optimized for Windows 95/98/NT.

Many practitioners get away with the minimalist approach for case management systems. They merely want to track critical dates in some sort of calendar and 10 to 20 other pieces of matter information which they can customize inside another related application such as time & billing. For this approach, see the integration of systems like Abacus® and Timeslips®.

Accounting Software

1. Time & Billing. What does time and billing software have to do with trial preparation? Ask the lawyer who has had to prove fees in court. There are increasing numbers of statutes allowing the prevailing party to assess lawyer's fees. In order to do that you will need a detailed (and often, contemporaneous) record of the work performed. The last thing you want to do after winning at trial is to have to go back through your files and appointment records in order to create a detailed bill.

   The market place is increasingly requiring lawyers to keep track of their time for accountability purposes as well. Many corporate clients are employing legal audit techniques, not only to review bills, but also to gather the empirical data on what it typically takes to process cases. The insurance industry is leading the pack on this, requiring defense counsel to detail their bills according to litigation codes, not unlike the diagnostic codes deployed in the medical profession. At a minimum, the time data will justify the bill for the work performed. It might also demonstrate whether or not the outcome of the case was worth all the effort.

One of the most popular time and billing applications on the market today is also one of the most affordable. The Sage US Corporation manufactures Timeslips. It can be accessed via the web at www.timeslips.com. An alternative is Juris by Juris Corporation, www.juris.com. Juris offers a time/expense tracking system that is integrated with accounts payable check writing and general ledger accounting. The other popular time and billing package is Tabs III by Software Technology, Inc. Tabs III combines various modules that allow integration of time and billing with case management, general ledger and trust accounting. They can be accessed at www.stilegal.com.

The key to buying any time and billing software is looking for ease of use and the ability to export and import data in open format (ASCII text, comma separated value, or CSV format). Often you will find a requirement by a client or a court for a copy of your billing records in an electronic format. If the system can export the data in an ASCII CSV format, you will have little problem exporting it into another database or spreadsheet program. That way the recipient can do further analysis on the bills as needed.

2. Accounts Payable. As long as you have to keep track of client funds and pay expert witness fees, you ought to consider keeping your firm's financial data all in a generally acceptable accounting system, especially if the system is easy to use and only costs a few hundred dollars. Depending on the time and billing software that you own, you may or may not have an integrated accounts payable/accounts receivable system. Given the relative cost of automating your check writing and trust accounting systems, it should be one of your higher priorities. Especially if you are in a jurisdiction that has strict client/lawyer trust fund accounting rules.

At the end of the year, the beauty of an accounts payable system is that all you have to do is print several reports in order to have various financial analyses ready to go to your accountant. If you ever want to know how much you spend on library/research or expert witness fees at the press of a button (or two), you must operate an accounts payable application. Point your browser at www.quickbooks.com in order to see QuickBooks Pro, one of the more affordable and popular general ledger/ accounts payable applications.

Document Preparation

1. <u>Word Processing.</u> We have gone way beyond the simple virtues of cut and paste, font control, letterheads and merging data files into the era where your word processor will automatically recognize legal and web citations. Gone are the days where you have to type a separate table of authorities in a brief; gone are the days of manually checking citations for proper Blue Book format, and gone are the days of manually shepardizing. For a good source of relevant and up-to-date tips and tricks on word processing, go to <u>www.abanet.org/lpm/newsletters/wp/home.html</u>.

   Modern Windows based word processors are designed to work with a variety of third party citation tools in order to check your citation format, generate table of authorities and even verify citations. See, for example, free tools offered by the West Group at, <u>www.westgroup.com/products/software</u>. Once downloaded and installed, they will add these automatic features to your word processor. Just be careful to understand the costs associated with using those components, such as Key Cite, which require logging onto the Internet based sites for Westlaw in order to perform the citation verification process.

   The modern versions of word processors (versions MS Word 95 and 97 and WordPerfect 8 and 9) can read and convert (save as) into each other's format. Today, you should try to save your documents as a RTF (rich text format). That is a "cross platform" format that will preserve your document formatting. In the not too distant future, the default format will be the native format of the Internet, HTML. This will enable a universal communication of information, both inside the document with citations as well as the document itself. Once you have an authentication mechanism for your work product (beyond the scope of this chapter, but known as a Digital Signature) get ready for electronic filing of those pleadings!

2. <u>Document Assembly.</u> The automated assembly of documents is the Holy Grail for many lawyers. Wouldn't it be nice to have all those pleadings, letters, and discovery materials automatically produced for you? Don't hold your breath. While there is wonderful technology for the building of such systems, they still require the time consuming work of building the logic and crafting the variable text. Document assembly systems are typically deployed in transactional-based law practices. One either buys a canned system or one where the lawyer has to build the system.

Legal vendors are increasingly selling forms on disk. Some are just plain forms and others are based on document assembly technology. To the extent that a busy trial lawyer needs to rely on commercial forms for document drafting, you should check the most recent listings of your law book vendor. A word to the wise is important; form books and document assembly systems (be they electronic or paper) only produce good first drafts. The lawyer should still review the document before committing to a final draft.

One of the most popular document assembly applications sold today is HotDocs, by the CapSoft Development Corporation, (www.capsoft.com). Other well known document assembly engines are ExpertText by Expertext Systems, Ltd., (www.expertext.com) and WinDraft by Eidelman Associates (http://www.lawtech.com/windraft). Another source of information about document assembly systems is at the Law Practice Management web site, www.abanet.org/lpm/newsletters/wp/home.html.

3. <u>Document Management.</u> Imagine the power of converting your file room to an electronic version. All of a sudden, the information stored away in case files can be instantly accessed. This provides a tremendous resource for precedent, work product retrieval, enhanced conflict of interest analysis ("where did I ever hear that name?") and information management.

There are two approaches to document management systems. One provides a structured database underneath each document. When a user creates a document, they are required to fill in an index card, or database structure containing basic bibliographic information about the document. The other approach is to deploy a full text retrieval system that reads and indexes every word in every document. This enables a Boolean, full text search and retrieval function, similar to a LEXIS or Westlaw search.

The latter approach can be accomplished for little money. The Isys Information and Management Retrieval system by Odyssey Development, Inc., (www.isysdev.com) is one such cost-effective application. Other products to look at are Sonar (Virginia Systems, Inc.), ZyIndex (Zylab International), or FolioViews (Open Market, Inc.). WordPerfect has a built-in version, known as Quick Finder. Microsoft provides a similar full text search tool with their Windows 95/98 operating system, known as Find Fast. But these built-in full text retrieval products are typically hard to use and product specific—they only read and index the files produced by their native application. Isys has become so popular because it is easy to use and it will read over 40 different file formats. There is also a web version, which many courts are beginning to use.

The more expensive document manager programs now combine database technology with full text retrieval systems. The popular systems on the market today are PC DOCS by PC DOCS, Inc., (www.pcdocs.com), WorldDOX (www.worldox.com), and iManage, by NetRight Technologies, Inc., (www.netright.com). Each of these companies' products also deals with version control as well as universal file naming conventions, so as to enable these systems to also work on the World Wide Web.

Legal Research

At the end of the twentieth century, lawyers find themselves between two research worlds, books and computers. Clearly, both have their virtues. Although you would be hard pressed to challenge the speed and efficiency of computer assisted legal (and fact) research (CALR), individuals who are more comfortable with the traditional legal research methods of the law library and with having a book in front of them can be just as competent (if not more so) to find the law. Yet for speed and efficiency, nothing beats the computer. For example, tracing the status of a case citation (Shepardizing or KeyCiting) just cannot be done as efficiently the old fashioned way, or imagine trying to find all the cases where a particular federal judge has commented on first amendment issues. It would be fairly routine to accomplish this with a CALR search across the appropriate Federal case database. It could take you days to do it the old-fashioned way.

The major legal publishers now give access to their information systems through the Internet. You can find Westlaw at www.westlaw.com, and LEXIS at www.lexis.com. Both the West Group (a division of Thompson

Corporation) and LEXIS/NEXIS (a division of Reed Elsevir, PLC) are in the process of converting their vast collection of legacy data into the format of the Internet document, or HTML. By doing so, you will be able to use a new parallel, electronic form of citation inside your work product, which will enable instant retrieval of those cites while inside the word processor. This technology is already enabled inside versions of WordPerfect for Windows, version 8 and up, and inside Microsoft Word for Windows, versions 95 and up.

In addition to the traditional online sources of legal information the Internet has become an alternative for finding primary legal materials such as legislative history, statutes, regulations, and even case law. Although it is not annotated or integrated to a comprehensive research system like Westlaw, it can sometimes be more current, accessible, and complementary. Take a look at all the information at www.thomas.gov.

All Federal law since 1995 is documented and accessible for free on the Internet. State after state is following suit. Florida, one of the more progressive state governments with respect to implementing a comprehensive Internet strategy, even publishes all of the state Supreme Court arguments in a Real Video/Audio format. You can also download the parties' briefs. For a view of where it is all heading in courthouse automation go to www.fsu.org/gavel2gavel and click on the courts' calendar to drill down to an argument. You will need to have a free piece of software loaded called the RealPlayer from www.real.com.

Research on the Internet can still be a bit unwieldy, but once you understand how to approach it you will find yourself increasingly using it, perhaps first to augment your traditional legal research, but soon you will find it becoming an indispensable, if not, primary resource.

General Research

The Law Practice Management section of the ABA has published several excellent books on the subject of using the Internet for legal and fact research: *Law on the Internet, The Best Legal Web Sites and More* by Eric J. Heels and Richard P. Klau; *The Internet Fact Finder for Lawyers* by Joshua D. Blackman and David Jank; and *The Complete Internet Handbook for Lawyers* by Jerry Lawson. You can find these and other titles at www.abanet.org/lpm/catalog.

The Internet has spawned a number of virtual law libraries that point to primary and secondary legal materials. Most are the results of law schools putting together a list of legal links. Bar associations and government agencies are also getting into the act, putting up web pages that point to primary legal source materials. Some of the more mature sites to begin your Internet legal research are located on web servers at the Cornell, Villanova, Emory, Washington and Lee, and Rutgers University law schools. See, for example, www.law.cornell.edu, www.law.emory.edu, www.law.indiana.edu/v-lib/lawindex.html, and www.lib.uchicago.edu/libInfo/law/.

There is also a growing list of "metasearch" sites, which contain search engines that execute your search among a specific set of web sites—in this case, specifically designed for law. See for example, FindLaw at www.find-law.com or Hieros Gamos at www.hg.org. Those are free sites, paid for by advertisers. LOIS, the Law Office Information Service, maintains one of the most comprehensive and affordable sites for legal research at www.loislaw.com. A similar company competing against the huge legal publishers is VersusLaw. Their site is at www.versus.com.

If you are not intimidated, you can try a keyword search through one of the general Internet search engines such as AltaVista, Lycos, or Yahoo. One way to approach a search like this is through the meta search engines www.all4one.com or www.dogpile.com. These will take your keyword search and simultaneously run it on four or more search engines. They then display the results simultaneously. This is one of the most efficient ways to run a keyword search on the Internet. It is also an instructive exercise in order to see what comes back when you search across the entire Internet as opposed to a "slice" dedicated to the law.

Internet-based e-mail conferences, known as list servs, cover hundreds of legal issues from adoption, divorce, legal ethics, international banking, intellectual property, technology in litigation, and on and on. These have become virtual communities where lawyers and other legal professionals (not to mention clients, so be careful what you post!) from around the world post questions and answers to the various issues confronting their practices. For one of the most comprehensive lists, go to www.lib.uchicago.edu/cgi-bin/law-lists. Also check out your bar association. The Association of Trial Lawyers of America (ATLA) maintains several list servs at www.atla.org. This is an excellent way to share ideas, cites, pleadings, motions, war stories, and information on expert witnesses.

Many of the sites mentioned above also contain sections and links to expert witness and fact investigation sites. Examples of these are at www.findlaw.com/13experts/index.html, www.expertwitness.com, and www.knowx.com (for a one-stop source for investigative resources).

Anyone preparing for trial who failed to search the Internet for information relating to issues of fact, information about expert witness', and even issues of law, runs the risk of failing to prepare their case with due diligence.

Litigation Support

Litigation support applications involve the use of database, full text retrieval and imaging systems to help organize the documents and transcripts produced in the life of a litigated matter. It was often felt that these applications were only cost justified in the most complex and voluminous of cases. With the advent of PC based computing, that attitude has changed.

Although there are a growing number of such programs, the real advantage of them all lies in the basic bibliographic document abstract. If you abstract each and every document for such basic information as document date, title, document type, author, recipient, Bates numbers, exhibit number, and the like, you will gain tremendous control and insight into the document population. As you use the system, you might decide to add a few more fields to the document database abstract in order to find and retrieve evidence on issues of law or fact.

The power of the database lies not only in the speed at which you can retrieve information (documents), but in the ability to pick categories of documents and then to sort them. Imagine abstracting hundreds or thousands of checks and invoices involved in a commercial dispute. Your document abstract might include fields for amount, payee, and invoice number. You could then do a search for all checks sorted by amount or date or payee. When you are looking at hundreds of records sorted in those different ways, you will be seeing patterns of information. Properly set up, the document database can not only save you hundreds of hours of time searching and retrieving evidence, but it can aid you qualitatively in terms of insights into the evidence.

The most popular litigation support packages on the market today combine the database functions with full text retrieval systems. That way you can do full text, Boolean searches across those documents of a full text nature (transcripts and work product such as pleadings), motions and affidavits, as well as the structured or fielded information in the database. These systems typically sell for under $1,000 per user. Summation, Concordance, In Magic, Replica and E-Binder are some of the packages out there. For further information, see www.lcsweb.com/software/index or the individual manufacturer's sites.

Transcript Management

Deposition and trial transcripts almost always exist in electronic format before they are printed to paper. You should make every effort to obtain all your transcripts on disc in a standard ASCII file format. You can then import the transcript into one of the commercial search engines or litigation support applications referred to above. DiscoveryZX (Stenograph Corp), Summation (Summation, Inc.), E-Transcript and E-Binder (PubNETics), and LiveNote FT (Livenote, Inc.) are products designed specifically to help you search, digest, and print condensed transcripts. Unlike other full text documents, transcripts have page and line, volume and date information that is critical to maintain in exact conformity with the official paper versions. When you are in trial and you find impeachable prior testimony on your computer, you had the best be assured that it conforms to the actual volume, date, page and line numbers of the official, signed transcript before the court!

The latest trend in transcripts has been to receive them "real time" and then synchronize the finished text with the video of the testimony. That means the spoken word appears on your computer screen (as well as the opposing counsel and judge's screens) with a minimal delay of a few seconds. During the course of a deposition or trial, you can "quick mark" or "issue code" specific testimony, search, and instantly play it back to check the testimony. You could even have the transcript distributed electronically through a modem for other lawyers or clients to review off site.

Ultimately the record of the testimony can be "synched" with the video and the complete digital copy recorded to disk (CD-ROM, a DVD, or a large hard drive). The most commonly used real time applications today are CaseView (Stenograph Corp.) and LiveNote FT (Livenote, Inc.). Because of the increasing popularity of this technology, other vendors are bringing products on line with even more sophisticated capabilities. One such vendor is LegalSpan (www.legalspan.net). Their @attend real time product uses the Internet to deliver RealVideo streams (www.real.com) and the real time transcript. You could receive this anywhere on the planet, as long as you have access to the Internet and the appropriate ID and password. With the capability of sending private chat and e-mail messages to the lawyer actually attending, you are virtually sitting as second chair.

Litigation Support on the Internet
There is an interesting new trend in litigation support systems which is to host all the data and images on a secure Internet web server. Known as a Litigation Extranet, the idea is to host the electronic equivalent of the case file on a secure web site that acts as a single, on line document repository. Access is "24x7" (24 hours a day, 7 days a week) and virtually from anywhere via an Internet web browser. It is very cost effective and easy to administer because it is essentially a basic, client-server style application.

The infrastructure of the Litigation Extranet is composed of the following packaged, cost effective Internet technologies:

1. <u>Client</u>—Web browsers: Netscape 4.+, Microsoft IE 4.+
2. <u>Server</u>—Web Server OS; MS NT/IIS, Linux/Apache
3. <u>Security</u>—SSL (secure socket layer), VPN(virtual private network).

In addition, the point, click, and retrieve attributes of the HTML language is an ideal format for lawyers because it permits efficient jumping to cited material and rapid access to litigation support functions such as links to documents, memos, research, people and calendar items, and enhanced communications (via e-mail, chat and message board systems). (See www.legalextranet.com.)

Trial Presentation

When all the preparation and organization is done, you are ready to go to court and try the case. Or, are you? Trying a case at the end of the Twentieth century is different than it was just five or ten years ago. And it will continue to change, in large part because the triers of fact are so different. Take a close look at the jury pool the next few times you go to court.

According to the noted trial and communications specialist, Sonya Hamlin everything in trial communication has changed. One of the most effective sources of information on this topic is in her book *What Makes Juries Listen*, available at www.legalwks.com. Juries are increasingly populated by younger and younger people, who want a faster presentation of information.

How can the solo practitioner or small law office compete? It has never been easier. Today's PC technology offers many different options for preparing visual exhibits. But like anything else, one can easily get distracted with the bells and whistles. Presentation technology like PowerPoint (Microsoft) or Freelance Graphics (IBM/Lotus), which in many cases came with the Office Suite of software you purchased when you bought your computer, has become a standard way of presenting to audiences. Use it. With a program like PowerPoint you can embed graphics, photographs, charts, and even movies.

Since most of us are not trained in graphic arts, it is important to test your presentation exhibits to a focus group of other lawyers and lay people before you take them to court. Also, make sure you show your exhibits to the opposing counsel and the judge at a pretrial conference in order to minimize last minute objections. Get those rulings done before the trial. You want the evidence to go in smoothly. And make sure the courtroom is set up to handle the electronic requirements of computer-based graphics.

If you think you need an expert to help you with the visual graphics, you will find many companies advertising such services on the web and in the local legal newspapers. Make sure the deliverables are in a format that you can work with (such as PowerPoint), assuming the need to make last minute changes, based on evidentiary rulings. One of the vendors in this area is Doar Communications (www.doar.com).

Ideally, when you are in court, you want to be able to access your evidence in an orderly and quick manner. If you have used a litigation support system and you have a database of all your documents with the associated images, then you have the ability to present the documents through an overhead projector or through a large screen computer monitor. Juries will increasingly expect to see this equipment.

Two companies from Arizona lead the market with trial presentation technology, inData (www.indatacorp.com) and Digital Practice, L.L.C. (www.digitalpractice.com). InData produces TrialDirector, which will link to your litigation support database and enable you to present images with either keystrokes or a barcode system. The TrialDirector product allows you to focus in (or zoom), then highlight or annotate parts of the image. Digital Practice, L.L.C., produces Trial-Link Express and Visionary, which similarly links to your litigation database and enables you to present multimedia, such as scanned documents, photos, charts, and even full motion MPEG video. Both of these companies have mature trial presentation products which are consistent with open system standards, so they will link to and import information from other systems.

The practice of law has never experienced as much change as it has today. With the appropriate understanding and use of technology, your advocacy should continue to meet the high standards of professionalism that clients expect. And you might just find that preparing for and trying that case can be fun, as well as exhausting.

Forms in Chapter 4

4 | Investigation

A complete initial investigation is critical to any litigation. With few exceptions (such as a statute of limitations problem), no lawsuit should be filed or defended on behalf of a client without a thorough investigation into the facts of the claim, the damages, and the defenses. The failure to conduct an adequate investigation prior to filing suit or responding can result in serious prejudice to the client, unnecessary friction with the client, and financial and other sanctions by the court against both lawyer and client.

Good initial investigation gives the trial lawyer the advantage in dealing with opposing counsel and other representatives of the opposition, as well as a clear edge in settlement negotiations or other critical positioning in the early stages of litigation. Moreover, documenting the facts while recollections are fresh may preclude some defenses or later changes.

The shape and extent of the initial investigation may vary widely depending on the nature of the case. Form 4–1 is a checklist for a motor vehicle (M.V.) accident case. Using this checklist as a guide, develop a similar list for the type of case you are handling, then sit down with your client and develop a checklist for the initial investigation in *your* case. Then work together to follow through on all items. Edit the list as more things come up, then you have your own fully developed checklist for the *next* case of that type.

The client should be involved, as far as practical, in the investigation, especially in obtaining the documents, and in otherwise participating in the handling of the case. However, the client should not be responsible for all of the investigation. The lawyer should control, direct, *document*, perform, and be accountable for the development of the case. To allow otherwise is to invite client dissatisfaction at best ("He didn't do anything; I had to do it all") and serious malpractice at worst.

Finally, in every phase of your investigation, put yourself in the other side's shoes: If you were representing them what would you be looking for? Include this perspective in your inquiries. It can be an invaluable tool: helping you to discover and anticipate problems, but also leading to inquiries that you might otherwise never have made.

I. Sources of Information

Client

The initial investigation always begins—and ends—with the client. He or she presumably knows the facts and documents best (at least from one perspective), has some of what you need at home or in the office, and can help you uncover and list other possible sources. Most successful litigation is a partnership between lawyer and client; however, many clients and many lawyers don't always realize this. You need to press your client repeatedly—verbally and in writing—to search his or her desk, files, and memory for any documents, information, witnesses, or leads that might help you develop the case.

Telephone

After the client, the second most underrated tool in a lawyer's initial investigation is the telephone. Lawyers who might call everywhere for information and documents on some new personal gadget, often forget how helpful the phone can be in a professional search for information. You will be surprised at how much can be learned in a litigation matter through the creative, persistent, and relentlessly polite use of the telephone, by you, an assistant, or even your client. One hint: always follow-up a call for information with a letter of thanks and a request for more information. The letter can be both a reminder and a prompt, and can be handled easily with a simple fill-in-the-blanks form letter.

Internet

The new best source of an enormous range of information is the Internet. Whether you are a veteran computer hacker and web cruiser or a computer dinosaur and web neophyte, there is a great deal of valuable material on the web that can help you in an initial investigation. Whether you do it yourself or enlist someone else's help, there are all kinds of resources for information on individuals, entities, issues, or whatever. (See Chapter 3.)

FOIA

Finally, don't forget that old government favorite, the Freedom of Information Act (FOIA) inquiry (5 USC § 552). Similar laws exist in many states. Follow-up *any* inquiry or lead to a government entity with an FOIA request. It is easy to do, and even if you think you already have everything, it is amazing how often the left hand of the bureaucracy does not know what the right hand is doing. The result can yield some pleasant surprises. However, be aware that the process can take a long time, and be prepared to follow-up every communication with telephone calls and confirming letters to press the urgency of your request.

Other

The range of possible sources for documents and information in an initial investigation can be extraordinarily broad. Other litigation, libraries, government agency records, news media, your colleagues, your client's colleagues, and many other avenues may be productive. Keep an open mind: the best information you may get from one source is an idea for *another* source. Follow the trail.

II. Document Collection and Review—Liability

Communications

Consider all possible forms of relevant communications—either to obtain now or to request in the future. Notice that the word is *communications,* not the old standby *correspondence.* Because of e-mail, voicemail, beepers, diaries, file memos, and every new and popular device, the world of communications has expanded considerably. Your creativity in investigating all sources of recorded information must expand accordingly.

Reports

Police reports, government reports, investigators' reports, annual reports, insurance company reports, and any other possible source of a report or compilation should be considered.

Photographs

Existing photographs (current and historical) of a person, a location, a piece of equipment or machinery, or other objects, places or phenomenon can come from many sources. These can include government agencies, media, architects, adjusters, investigators, employees, or other individuals or entities. They should be gathered and preserved right away for use in evaluating the case, presenting it, or even assisting or cross examining experts.

Other

Think creatively about what might help you to support, explain, or counter every aspect of the case, or provide you with helpful information about the other side or their witnesses. Begin the search for any and all such documents early, and keep at it through to the very end.

III. Document Collection and Review—Damages

Medical

Begin the process of seeking both clinical and billing records for *every* healthcare provider that had anything to do with the matter. Find out who they work for or with, then request their records. Make sure you get to see the originals: changes, white-outs, and other important information may not be readily apparent from copies.

Employment

A current personnel file is important, but it should only be the first step in reviewing employment records. What are the employer's personnel policies and practices? Do individual managers keep their own employee files? What is the compensation for comparable employees? Many more similar questions may arise. Then, this same level of detailed inquiry needs to be applied to prior jobs, with the added focus on why and how the employee left.

Financial

What are the money damages, depending on the type of case? Out-of-pocket losses? Lost income or interest? Lost profits? Lost opportunities? How do you evaluate the intangibles: punitive damages, pain and suffering, and so forth? What are the documents that might support, explain, or rebut?

Other

Again, think early, creatively, and aggressively about damages and what might be out there to support your arguments.

IV. Direct Investigation

Visits

There is usually no good substitute for a personal visit to help you understand a case. Whether it is an accident scene, a job site, a business, or whatever, how can you figure out how to make the case real to a jury if it is not real to you?

Consider going with your client, if possible, so you will have a good understanding of his or her perspective. If the case warrants an expert, try to visit with the expert. Take a camera whenever appropriate.

Experts / Private Investigators

Begin the search right away to get the help you need. The courts have greatly expanded the types of issues that can be the subject of expert testimony. Think about where such testimony might help your case and start looking for the right experts. Get referrals from your client, other lawyers, people in the particular profession, and any other sources, as well as considering the various referral agencies. If witness interviews, surveillance, or other affirmative investigation are called for, go through a similar process to find a good private investigator. Be clear about what you want, and keep a close watch on the process.

Witnesses

Unlike wine, witnesses' memories and testimony rarely get better with age. You need to move quickly to identify, find, and get written *signed* statements from every possible witness. Develop a form set of questions as reminders (See Forms 4–2 and 4–3). Remember, though, to be careful about speaking to nonclient witnesses alone: you risk putting yourself in the position of being the only witness if stories change or if part of the statement becomes an issue. In getting a witness statement, do not use terms such as "must have been," "probably," "maybe," "should have," "think," "seemed," and the like. These are not words of description. They are words of opinion. When they are uttered by a witness, a red flag should go up. Even if the witness is favorable to you, the testimony can be destroyed along with your case in cross-examination or at a deposition by a skillful cross-examiner. Push for the facts: who, what, when, why, where.

Damages

Consider ways of developing new evidence on damages, whether expert reviews, photos or videotape, reenactments, or other methods.

Other

Too often, lawyers treat cases passively: waiting for evidence to come to them through the normal discovery process. In most cases, you are not doing your job as a litigator if you do not actively investigate. This is, after all, a search for truth. Get out there and start searching.

V. Investigative Risks and Pitfalls

Advance Warning to the Other Side
In many types of cases, the other side does not know that you are seriously contemplating either bringing a suit or raising certain legal or factual issues as defenses or affirmative claims. You should carefully consider how to structure any investigation so as to avoid or delay disclosure or minimize its impact (for example, the other side creating or destroying documents, warning or preparing witnesses, other self-serving actions).

Advance Warning to Others
In some cases, your client is not the only person who could bring the same lawsuit: for example, whistleblower (Qui Tam) actions, shareholder actions, and other class actions could be initiated by people other than your client. Here again, reckless investigation can result in unwanted disclosure, causing your client to lose the "race to the courthouse."

Contacts with Represented Individuals
There are evolving local, state, and federal rules and cases on contacts with represented individuals that lawyers need to review carefully before conducting investigations. Among the most difficult areas are employees (or even former employees) of a party. Know the law in this area.

Lawyer as Witness
Every trial lawyer secretly yearns to be Sherlock Holmes (or some other great detective). However, the lawyer's true role as a courtroom advocate requires care and restraint in any investigative work. For example, if you interview a potential witness, you become a witness to what he or she said, if they are later uncooperative, contradicted, or unavailable. If you interview that witness *alone*, you become the only witness to what was said, which may limit your ability to use those statements at trial without crossing the line from lawyer to witness. You also have no back-up if the witness makes accusations about *your* words or conduct. Consider the implications carefully, and be very reluctant to interview witnesses alone.

Further Reading
Baldwin, Scott; Francis H. Hare, Jr.; and Francis E. McGovern. *The Preparation of a Products Liability Case*. Boston: Little, Brown and Company, 1981.

Friedman, Theodore H. *Pretrial Tactics and Techniques in Personal Injury Litigation.* Litigation and Administrative Practice Series. New York: Practicing Law Institute, 1980.

Frost, Harold A.; Marvin V. Ausubel. *Preparation of a Negligence Case.* Rev. ed. New York: Practicing Law Institute, 1967.

Preiser, *Stanley E. Preparation and Trial of a Neck and Back Sprain Case.* Belleville, Ill.: Trial Lawyers Service Co., 1966.

Shandell, Richard E. *The Preparation and Trial of Medical Malpractice Cases.* New York: Law Journal Seminar Press, 1981.

4-1 M.V. ACCIDENT INVESTIGATION CHECKLIST

I. Indirect Investigation.

    A. Liability.

        1. Accident report. This may contain some or all of the following:
           a. Time and details of accident.
           b. Response time.
           c. Weather and road conditions.
           d. Witnesses' names and addresses.
           e. Res gestae statements.
           f. Liability facts.
           g. Diagram of scene and location of vehicles.
           h. Complaints of injury at scene.
           i. Drivers' license numbers and restrictions.
           j. Citations issued with ticket number.

        2. Check sources for photographs of the scene, vehicle, and parties:
           a. Your client's own insurance company's adjuster.
           b. Adverse insurance company adjuster.
           c. Repairmen.
           d. Local, state and federal investigative agencies.
           e. Newspaper and TV studios.

        3. Adverse driver citation.
           a. If adverse driver pled guilty, obtain certified copy.
           b. If the traffic case is still pending, consider having a transcript made of the trial or arraignment.

        4. Adverse driver's driving record. May be certified by the state and thus self-authenticated for purposes of FRE 902.

        5. Vehicle registration and title. The accident report will have a tag number. Registration records are usually public and copies can be obtained from the state to verify ownership.

        6. Client's insurance policy. Get copy of client's entire policy. Consider claims for the following:
           a. Uninsured or underinsured motorist benefits.
           b. No-fault benefits.
           c. Medical payments benefits.
           d. Property damage/collision.

e. Rental or loss of use.

f. Other designated benefits.

7. Weather data. If an issue, get weather data from the National Climactic Center, NOAA, Asheville, NC, or other agencies.

8. Other investigative sources and records.
   a. Coroner's records in death cases and commitments.
   b. State industrial safety or accident commission.
   c. CAB and FAA reports in aviation accidents.
   d. U.S. Coast Guard and Harbor Police.
   e. Public utilities commission and Interstate Commerce Commission.
   f. Notices of violations/accidents to city, state, or federal agencies.
   g. Newspaper or TV accounts of incident.

B. Damages

1. Hospital records. Obtain a complete copy, including:
   a. The names of all admitting and consulting physicians, nurses, and other providers
   b. Complete daily record of medication and all vital signs (temperature, pulse, respiration).
   c. Lab-work results.
   d. Doctor's admission reports, progress notes, and discharge summaries.
   e. Nurses' notes that document your client's problems, complaints, mood, appetite, etc.
   f. X-rays and test results.

2. Doctor's reports. Obtain reports from treating physicians and other examining physicians to include the following:
   a. History.
   b. Complaints.
   c. Examination, tests and findings
   d. Diagnosis.
   e. Prognosis.
   f. Evaluation of disability and permanency.

3. Life expectancy.
   a. Mortality tables.
   b. Actuary.

4. Funeral, burial, and medical bills. Prosthesis and physical aids expenses.

5. Repair bills or estimates. Obtain repair bills or estimates and rental car expenses and loss-of-use documentation.

6. Wage loss and tax records.
   a. Client's tax returns, from client or IRS.
   b. Current earnings for year to date (check stubs).
   c. Employer statement on time and earnings lost.
   d. Fringe benefits and pension-type plans.
   e. Future loss of earnings (economist as resource).

7. Sources of information.
   a. Standards and rules for industry or activity.
      1) Statutes and agency regulations.
      2) Association, industry, or company standards.
      3) American Standards Association codes and manuals.
   b. Technical literature.
   c. Lay literature—magazines, newspapers.
   d. Experts in industry.
   e. Government agency investigation reports and publications.

II. Direct Investigation

A. Liability.

1. Visit to scene. Observe and note:
   a. How the intersection is controlled in all directions.
   b. Speed limit and other reduce-speed signs.
   c. Stop and yield signs.
   d. Lane divisions (if any).
   e. Crosswalks, pedestrian control signs, stop bars.
   f. Traffic control signals, and timing and sequence.
   g. Road conditions.
   h. Skid and gouge marks.
   i. Obstructions to vision for both vehicles.
   j. Other factors.

2. Photographs of scene and vehicles.
   a. Scene.
      1) Photograph from all angles and lines of sight, including that of the adverse party. Consider aerial photos.
      2) Investigate sources for photographs by others of occurrence or scene.
   b. Vehicle.
      1) Show the violence inside the automobile.
      2) Exterior shots should include all four sides of the vehicle, even if undamaged.

3) Pay attention to the interior glass, the steering wheel, and any component evidencing impact by the occupants.

4) Photograph hair and blood when present.

3. Locating witness statements. Locate witnesses and statements through:
   a. Accident reports.
   b. Client statements.
   c. Witness statements.
   d. Neighborhood canvas, including letter carrier, shopkeepers, delivery people.
   e. Newspaper accounts.
   f. Adverse party statement.
   g. Investigation officers, judicial proceedings, coroner's inquest, hospital emergency room records.

4. Content of witness statements.
   a. What the witness was doing before the accident.
   b. Where he was looking.
   c. Why he was looking there ("I was waiting for the light to change so I could cross the street").
   d. What actually brought his attention to the accident.
   e. What he saw, in "super slow motion" detail.
   f. Ask the witness to sketch a diagram of the scene and the accident.

B. Damages.

1. Photographs of client. Record observable injuries to be used as trial exhibits. Consider videotape of a day in the life of a client with a permanent disability.

2. Daily diary of client activities, complaints and treatment.
   a. Compare with activities before accident.
   b. Prove loss of enjoyment of life.
   c. Bring in lay witnesses.

4-2 LAY WITNESS INFORMATION

Your Name: _____

Your Address: _____

Age: _____ Marital status:_____

Phone Office: _____ Home: _____ E-mail :_____

Occupation: _____

Education: _____

Employment history: _____

_____

_____

Special achievements or honors (don't be modest): _____

_____

How long have you known plaintiff, and in what context have you known him/her?
(neighbor, worked together): _____

_____

_____

What were preinjury activities of plantiff? (sport, work around the house, type of
work): _____

_____

_____

First knowledge of injury to plantiff: _____

_____

_____

Describe what you observed about the plantiff that changed after the injury. (Give specific examples if possible—stopped bowling, face showed tension, pain.) _____

_____

_____

How often did you see plantiff after injury? Be as specific as possible. _____

_____

_____

What did you know of plaintiff's personal life with family and friends? (Summarize)

_____

_____

_____

_____

_____

Please add any comments of your own. _____

_____

_____

_____

_____

Describe what you observed about the plantiff that changed after the injury. (Give specific examples if possible—stopped bowling, face showed tension, pain.)

In regard to appearance: _____

_____

In regard to work missed, work difficulties: _____

_____

_____

In regard to recreational activities: _____

_____

_____

In regard to home activities (No more gardening, sewing, lawn care): _____

_____

_____

4-3 EYEWITNESS STATEMENT

My name is _____

My address is _____

My phone number is _____

I am/am not related to or acquainted with any of the parties involved in the accident.

I have previously made statements regarding the accident to

_____

To the best of my knowledge and recollection, the accident

was at _____ on _____

at approximately _____ o'clock.

At that time I was _____

_____

_____

_____

_____

Prior to the accident, I observed the following: _____

_____

_____

_____

During the accident, I observed the following: _____

_____

_____

_____

After the accident, I observed the following: _____

_____

_____

_____

Other observations and comments: _____

_____

_____

_____

Signed _____

5 | Preliminary Procedural Matters and Filing Suit

I. Legal Theories

After the client interview, initial investigation, and necessary legal research are conducted, the lawyer must decide what legal theories will apply in the prosecution or defense of the case. The theories relied upon may determine the type of evidence admissible and the amount of recovery. While it may be possible to change theories during litigation, do not assume that the court will allow an amendment to the pleadings before trial to accommodate a change in the theory of the case.

Damages in a civil suit may include claims not only for compensatory damages, punitive damages and interest, but also for attorneys' fees. Both federal and state statutes should be examined to see if attorneys' fees may be awarded. Attorneys' fees may be recoverable in cases where the client does not recover monetary damages but is successful in preserving or protecting individual rights granted by contract, statute, or constitution.

Where immediate results are required, the lawyer may have only a short time to consider the legal theories available for recovery, as in a case with statute of limitations problems or where injunctive relief is sought to prevent imminent harm to a client's person or property. If a cursory evaluation of an equity case indicates that a damage claim may also be viable, file the initial lawsuit for injunctive relief and explore additional legal theories for damages when the immediate problem is resolved.

In addition to the legal theories of the case, consider also the miscellaneous legal issues that often arise in litigation and can affect the outcome of the case. Consideration of these issues early on will minimize surprises, shape the course of the litigation, and may ultimately affect the outcome of the lawsuit. For example:

- In a dram shop action, will the amount of the recovery be limited by statute?
- In a death case, will punitive damages be available in the survival action?
- What problems of proof will arise in establishing the existence of an agency relationship as opposed to a defendant's claim to having the status of an independent contractor?
- Does the economic loss doctrine limit the action to a claim for breach of contract rather than allowing a tort action?
- Does privity exist in a case for breach of warranty?

The following is a checklist of some common legal theories of recovery and miscellaneous legal issues that may arise in the course of the litigation:

A. Theories for recovery at law.
    1. Personal injury actions.
        a. General negligence.
        b. Premises liability.
        c. Products liability.
        d. Professional negligence.
        e. Dram shop action.
        f. FELA/Federal Tort Claims Act/Jones Act.
        g. Municipal liability.
        h. Worker's compensation claim.
        i. Negligent entrustment.
    2. Miscellaneous tort actions.
        a. Tortious interference with a contract.
        b. Libel/slander.
        c. Misappropriation
        d Bad faith.
        e. Intentional torts.
        f. Negligence.
        g. Fraud/misrepresentation.
    3. Breach of contract/warranty actions.
        a. Actual or prospective breach.
        b. Actual or implied warranty.
        c. Consumer Protection (State/Federal Laws).
        d. Debt Collection practices (State/Federal Laws)

    4. Employment and related actions.
       a. Wrongful termination.
       b. Discrimination (age, sex, race).
       c. ADA.
       d. ERISA.
       e. Whistleblower (Qui Tam).
       f. Noncompete or Confidentiality.

B. Damages potentially recoverable in tort or contract claims.
    1. Compensatory damages.
    2. Punitive damages.
    3. Lawyers' fees.
    4. Interest.
    5. Impaired earning capacity.
    6. Future medical expenses.
    7. Lost profits.
    8. Other losses within the reasonable contemplation of the parties.

C. Theories for equitable relief.
    1. Injunction.
    2. Rescission.
    3. Reformation.
    4. Mandamus.
    5. Specific performance.

D. Miscellaneous legal issues.
    1. Agency/independent contractor relationship.
    2. Economic loss doctrine.
    3. Comparative negligence/contributory negligence.
    4. Contribution/indemnity.
    5. Potential third-party claims.
    6. Mandatory arbitration prior to filing suit.
    7. Governmental or charitable immunity.
    8. Court of claims disposition only.
    9. Limitation by state of damages recoverable.
    10. Pending legislation or cases.
    11. Applicability of possible affirmative defenses, for example, laches, statute of frauds, illegality, satisfaction.
    12. Privity of contract.
    13. Assumption of risk.
    14. Medical and legal causation.

II. Related Considerations

Ability to Recover

An early effort should be made to identify all possible defendants, including all primary and secondary defendants, and to determine whether the defendant is insured or has sufficient monetary assets to pay the potential judgment in full or in part. This can frequently be determined by a simple phone call to the adjuster handling the file or through some informal investigation. The amount of insurance is also important, especially in cases of catastrophic injury. It is much better to find out early if the amount of insurance available is inadequate to compensate the client for the injuries or property damage sustained. Knowing from the beginning of the case gives the lawyer a head start in locating alternative sources of compensation.

In the absence of a solvent defendant or adequate insurance coverage, the lawyer should investigate the client's uninsured or underinsured coverage. If it is determined that there simply is no source of recovery, tell the client.

It is also advisable to determine whether more than one person or entity may be liable. Multiple defendants may be separately or jointly liable in tort. Identifying all possible defendants early in the investigation could be useful where one of the defendants is inadequately insured or lacks assets sufficient to satisfy an anticipated judgment. Identifying and learning as much about defendants can also be useful in evaluating the case and developing litigation strategies. When possible, obtain any public records available regarding a defendant or consult newspapers or other publications which might contain valuable information about the defendants.

Filing of Notice of Claim

In many jurisdictions, advance notice of the filing of certain types of cases is a prerequisite before a lawsuit can be filed. Most statutes and government contracts requiring the prior filing of a notice of claim are exacting as to the manner and method that the notice has to be made. Mechanic's liens statutes are often very precise as to when and upon whom a notice of the claim for lien must be served and filed, the content of the claim for lien itself, and the lawsuit to protect the lien. Similar requirements may be made by statutes in tort actions or by contract in construction litigation involving governmental entities. Do not ignore statutory or contractual requirements that specific information about how the claim must be served upon a designated official. When in doubt as to whether the notice should be made by regular mail, certified mail, registered mail with receipt request, or by personal service, use all available methods to eliminate any doubt as to compliance with the contractual or statutory requirements.

Statute of Limitations

1. Running of statute. The applicability of the pertinent statute of limitations for the action in question is of vital importance. This is especially true in claims, such as mechanic's liens, where the claimant waits until the last possible moment to obtain payment before turning his claim over to a lawyer. Regardless of the type of case, knowing the statute of limitations should be the first issue considered. Generally, the limitation period for filing a specific action is found in the limitations of actions chapter in the state statutes; however, it may be necessary to consult other statutes as well. For example, the time period allowed for filing a will-contest action or renouncing the will itself is often covered in the probate act. If the statute of limitations period has run on the legal action contemplated, the attorney must consult the local rules on interruption of the statute to determine if the time for taking the required legal course of action has been extended.

2. Interruption of Statute of Limitations.
   a. Many states have now adopted some form of a discovery rule by either case law or statute that postpones the accrual date of a statute of limitations until the cause of action is or should have been known. Common examples include:
      1) Toxic tort litigation in which a claimant's illness may not develop until several years after the initial exposure.
      2) Medical malpractice actions in which the adverse consequences from a negligent diagnosis or surgical procedure may not be apparent for several years after the negligent act was committed.
      3) Construction litigation in which damage to a building does not become manifest until several years after defective material was used.
      4) Causes involving sexual abuse.
   b. A statute of limitations also may be tolled temporarily because of a plaintiff's legal disability. The accrual date of the cause of action commences when the legal disability is removed. Legal disability may arise when a plaintiff is:

1) In prison.
2) Mentally incompetent, or otherwise incapacitated.
3) Absent from the state.
4) A minor.

c. You may also be able to overcome the tolling of a statute of limitations in the following ways:
   1) Recharacterize theory of case from personal injury to contract, statute.
   2) Sue in equity for collateral remedies.
   3) Assert claim as setoff or counterclaim.
   4) Accrual at time of last exposure to substance.
   5) Continuing negligence theory.
   6) Fraud—accrual at discovery of fraud.
   7) Concealment of cause of action—fraud, or concealed in fiduciary relationship.
   8) Plaintiff's blameless ignorance or mistake.
   9) Apply statute of foreign state under statutory cause of action.
   10) Resist application of borrowing statute by strict interpretation of terms.
   11) Defendant is a foreign corporation not registered.
   12) Estoppel.
   13) Join with joint tortfeasor.
   14) Add new theory by amendment.

III. Jurisdiction

Federal

1. <u>Federal Question.</u> Federal District courts have original jurisdiction of all civil actions arising under the constitution, laws, or treaties of the United States, 28 USC § 1331. There is no requirement of a minimum amount in controversy for jurisdiction on this basis. Other subject matters in which Congress has provided jurisdiction to federal district courts include:

    a. Admiralty, maritime, and prize cases. 28 USC § 1333.
    b. Bankruptcy cases and proceedings. 28 USC § 1334.
    c. Interpleader. 28 USC § 1335.
    d. Enforcement or review of orders of the Interstate Commerce Commission. 28 USC § 1336.
    e. Commerce and antitrust regulations. 28 USC § 1337.

    f. Patents, copyrights, trademarks, and unfair competition. 28 USC § 1338.

    g. Postal matters. 28 USC § 1339.

    h. Internal Revenue and customs duties. 28 USC § 1340.

    i. Civil rights violations. 28 USC § 1343.

    j. Election disputes. 28 USC § 1344.

    k. United States as a plaintiff. 28 USC § 1345.

    l. United States as a defendant. 28 USC § 1346.

    m. Partition action where the United States is joint tenant. 28 USC § 1347.

    n. Clients action for a tort. 28 USC § 1350.

    o. Consuls, vice-consuls, and members of a diplomatic mission as defendants. 28 USC § 1351.

    p. Indian allotments. 28 USC § 1353.

    q. Land grants from different states. 28 USC § 1354.

    r. Fines, penalties, or forfeitures incurred under federal law. 28 USC § 1355.

    s. Injurics under federal laws. 28 USC § 1347.

    t. Eminent domain. 28 USC § 1358.

    u. ERISA. Claims regarding employee benefit plans, including employee group health and life insurance policies. 29 USC § 1144.

    v. False Claims Act Qui Tam (whistleblower) actions.

2. <u>Diversity jurisdiction.</u> 28 USC § 1332. Jurisdiction based on diversity depends upon the citizenship of the parties and not the subject matter in dispute. In order for there to be diversity jurisdiction, it must be complete. This means that each party on one side of the lawsuit must be a citizen of a state different from each party on the opposing side. For the purpose of determining diversity jurisdiction, the citizenship of an individual is determined to be its domicile and not merely residence. Various rules also apply in establishing the citizenship of a corporate defendant. Diversity is determined at the time of the commencement of the action and is not affected if one of the parties has a subsequent change of citizenship. The amount in controversy must exceed the sum or value of $75,000 exclusive of interest and costs, and there must be an actual controversy in existence as opposed to a potential legal dispute. Furthermore, even though the requirements of diversity jurisdiction may have otherwise been met, the court will decline jurisdiction in certain areas such as domestic relations and probate.

Additional issues pertaining to diversity jurisdiction that the lawyer should consider include:

a. the authority of the court to realign the parties.
b. removal of cases from state to federal court. 28 USC §§ 1441–52
c. strategies to defeat diversity jurisdiction.
d. class actions.
e. the determination of citizenship of natural persons, corporations, and business associations.

State

1. <u>Subject Matter Jurisdiction.</u> Before a court can entertain a lawsuit, it must have the power or authority to determine the legal issues in the case. The authority that a state court has to act is usually founded upon the state's constitution. However, some states are adopting mandatory arbitration rules or other alternatives for cases involving smaller dollars or other issues. It is important to consult with the applicable rules of civil procedure and court rules in effect to determine what type of case may be filed and what procedural requirements must be complied with before the court has the power to hear the case.

   All states also have some type of administrative review procedure pertaining to the power of trial courts to review decisions made by administrative agencies. Decisions made by zoning boards, road districts, and other governmental bodies normally cannot be ruled upon by a trial court until all avenues of review have been exhausted. If the claim involves some administrative action in which a client's property or money is at stake, it is important not to simply run to the courthouse and threaten litigation but rather to be certain to comply with all preliminary procedural requirements to be certain that the trial court does have jurisdiction over the subject matter in question. Finally, it is important to note that cases involving actions against the state for personal injury or otherwise frequently may be limited to filing in a state's court of claims.

2. <u>Personal Jurisdiction.</u> Once it is determined that the court has subject matter jurisdiction, it must then be decided whether the court has in personal jurisdiction over the person of the defendant and/or in re jurisdiction over property. Each state has its own rules with regard to procedural requirements that must be met in cases involving

attachment, garnishment, replevin, and similar actions and also has rules pertaining to the manner and method in which a defendant can be served. The states also have long-arm statutes or civil rules that set forth the jurisdiction state courts have over defendants who commit certain acts within the state. These statutes or rules are based on the existence of "minimum contacts" that the defendant has with the state. When there is some question as to the validity of personal jurisdiction based on a state's long-arm statute, it is worthwhile to refer to case law on the subject, for example., *World-wide Volkswagen Corp. v. Woodson*, 444 U.S. 286 (1980), and *Asahi Metal Industry Co., Ltd. v. Superior Court*, 480 U.S. 102, 107 S. Ct. 1026, 94 L. Ed 2d 92 (1987).

IV. Venue

Practical Considerations

Once it is determined that the Court has jurisdiction, the next question is where is the proper *venue*. Apart from the legal rules that apply in deciding the venue of a case, considerations should be given to practical aspects that may affect the course of the litigation or perhaps the outcome of the trial. In personal injury cases, for example, there may be a potentially higher verdict in an urban area, but it usually takes longer to get to trial. If you are unfamiliar with the trends and verdicts in a particular jurisdiction, it is usually wise to contact a local lawyer for an opinion.

Venue by Nature of the Case

Many states have statutes or civil rules that specify the county in which an action must be brought. For example, actions for replevin and attachment must be filed in the county where the property is located. Will contests usually must be filed in the county where the decedent died. In family cases the state's statute or civil rules usually specify the county in which a petitioner may file the action and what the requirements are for obtaining residency or domicile. Special rules often apply for members of the armed services. Most states have now adopted the Uniform Child Custody Jurisdiction Act, which controls venue in child custody disputes.

Federal Court

1. <u>Action based on diversity jurisdiction.</u> In a civil action where jurisdiction is based on the diversity of citizenship of the parties, the

case may be brought in the judicial district where all the plaintiffs or all the defendants reside or in which the claim arose. 28 USC § 1391a.

2. Actions not based solely on diversity. In a civil action in which jurisdiction is not based solely on diversity of citizenship of the parties, the action may be brought only in the judicial district where all defendants reside or in which the claim arose, except as otherwise provided by law. 28 USC § 1391b.

3. United States as a defendant. A civil action in which the defendant is an officer, an employee, or agency of the United States may be brought in any judicial district in which (a) a defendant in the action resides, (b) the cause of action arose, (c) any real property involved in the action is situated, or (d) the plaintiff resides if no real property is involved in the action. 28 USC § 1391e.

4. Corporations. A corporation may be sued in any judicial district in which it is incorporated or licensed to do business, or is doing business and such judicial district shall be regarded as the residence of the corporation. 28 USC § 1391c.

5. Defendants or property in different districts in the same state. Any civil action against defendants residing in different districts in the same state may be brought in any one of such districts. Also, any civil action involving the same property in different districts in the same state may also be brought in any one of such districts. 28 USC § 1392.

6. Venue where different divisions are involved. Any civil action against a single defendant and a district containing more than one division must be brought in the division in which the defendant resides. Actions against defendants residing in different divisions of the same district or different districts in the same state may be brought in any of such divisions. 28 USC § 1393.

7. Venue under federal statutes and laws. There are numerous federal statutes and laws that specify the proper venue in which a case may be filed. Some of the statutes include the following:
    a. Interpleader. 28 USC § 1335.
    b. Fine, penalty, or forfeiture. 28 USC § 1395.
    c. Internal revenue matters. 28 USC § 1396.
    d. Patents and copyrights. 28 USC § 4000.
    e. Stockholder's derivative action. 28 USC § 1401.
    f. United States as a defendant. 28 USC § 1402.
    g. Eminent domain. 28 USC § 1403.

In addition, some actions brought under specific federal laws by either the United States or private citizens have special venue provisions that control unfair labor practices, 29 USC § 116(j); antitrust violations, 15 USC § 1522; and Jones Act, 46 USC § 688.

8. <u>Change or transfer of venue.</u> A district court has the authority to transfer a civil action to any other district or division where it might have been brought "for the convenience of parties and witnesses" and in the interest of justice. 28 USC § 1404. The court normally has a wide discretion to make such a determination. Factors often considered by the court are the proximity of the witnesses of both the plaintiff and the defendant, the accessibility of evidence likely to be produced at trial, the power of the court to compel respective witnesses to testify at the trial, and court congestion. If the venue is improper, as opposed to being merely inconvenient, the court can either dismiss the action entirely or simply transfer the action to the correct forum. 28 USC § 1406.

9. <u>Venue in removal cases.</u> Proper venue for a case that is removed from state to federal court is in the district in which the state action is pending. 28 USC § 1446a.

Further Reading

Absence from the State as a Basis for Tolling the Statute of Limitations. *55 A.L.R. 3d* 1158.

Determination of a Corporation's Place of Business for Purposes of Diversity Jurisdiction. *6 A.L.R. Fed.* 611.

Federal Civil Procedure. *Corpus Juris Secundum* 2d §§ 186–223, §§ 464–516.

Federal Practice and Procedure. 32 *Am. Jur. 2d,* 1188–1253.

Forum Non-Conveniens in Product Liability Cases. *59 A.L.R. 3d* 138.

Imprisonment as a Basis for Tolling the Statute of Limitations. *59 A.L.R. 3d* 685.

Improper Venue Under 28 USC § 1406. 3 *A.L.R. Fed.* 476.

In Personal Jurisdiction Based on Contracts Made Within the State by a Non-resident or a Foreign Corporation. 23 *A.L.R. 3d* 551.

In Personal Jurisdiction in Products Liability Cases. 19 *A.L.R. 3d* 13.

In Personal Jurisdiction Over a Non-resident or Foreign Corporation for Commission of a Tort Within the State. 24 *A.L.R. 3d* 532.

Mechanic's Liens: Sufficiency of Notice, Claim or Statement of Mechanic's Lien. 48 *A.L.R. 3d* 153.

Modern Status of Law Requiring Notice of Tort Claims Against Local Government Entities. *59 A.L.R. 3d* 93.

Moore's Federal Practice. 2d ed. Vols. I, IA.

Notice Requirements to Hold Governmental Units Liable in Personal Injury Cases. 44 *A.L.R. 3d* 1108.

Pendent Jurisdiction Over Non-federal Claims. 5 *A.L.R. 3d* 1040.

Pleading Tactics as to Jurisdiction. 3 *Am Jur. Trials* 681–797.

Pleading Tactics as to Venue. 3 *Am. Jur. Trials.* 681–797.

Removal of Actions from State to Federal Court. 38 *A.L.R. Fed.* 824.

Selecting the Forum–The Defendant's Position. 3 *Am. Jur. Trials* 611.

Selecting the Forum–The Plaintiff's Position. 3 *Am. Jur. Trials* 555.

Statute of Limitations for Actions Based on Interference with a Contract. 58 *A.L.R. 3d* 1027.

Statute of Limitations for Actions Based on Strict Liability in Tort. 91 *A.L.R. 3d* 455.

Statute of Limitations for Attorney Malpractice. 2 *A.L.R. 4th* 284.

Statute of Limitations for Claims Involving Building Contracts. 1 *A.L.R. 3d* 914.

Statute of Limitations for Contribution Actions. 57 *A.L.R. 3d* 927.

Statute of Limitations for Dental Malpractice. 3 *A.L.R. 4th* 318.

Statute of Limitations for Indemnity Actions. 57 *A.L.R. 3d* 833.

Wright; Miller; and Cooper. *Federal Practice and Procedure.* 2d ed. §§ 3561–3868.

Forms in Chapter 6

6 | Pretrial Discovery

Discovery in the trial context is defined in *Black's Law Dictionary* as "the pre-trial devices that can be used by one party to obtain facts and information about the case from the other party in order to assist the party's preparation for trial." Of course, it is worth noting that even Black's goes on to say, "see also . . . Fishing trip or expedition."

The nature and extent of discovery are dictated by the facts and theories of each particular case. The purposes for which information is sought, type of information sought, amount in controversy, costs of litigation, potential problems in discovery, and availability of alternate sources of information will determine both the timing and extent of discovery. The general purposes of discovery are:

1. Uncover or confirm facts or evidence;
2. Minimize surprise;
3. Limit issues;
4. Lock in the other side's position;
5. Expedite settlement, summary judgment, or trial.

The permissible scope of discovery is generally very broad. It includes any matter relevant to issues in litigation and any facts that although irrelevant to issues by themselves may lead to admissible evidence.

Discovery is intended to be wide open and far-ranging, and courts tend to disfavor limitations and exclusions. However, they do exist and can become pivotal battles in the progress of a case. Note that in many jurisdictions, the party resisting discovery by asserting a privilege or other exclusion is required to demonstrate that the claimed privilege applies. These privileges may include:

1. Attorney-Client Privilege. We are all familiar with the one-on-one privilege, but issues of corporate counsel and other variations have added new challenges.
2. Accountant Privilege.
3. Health Care Providers.
4. Work Product / Trial Preparation material.

Factors that may indicate material is not work product:

1. Inherent nature of business or activities of preparer that makes preparation useful regardless of litigation.
2. Documents customarily prepared regardless of litigation.
3. Documents impartial—not adversarial in nature.
4. No attorney participation in preparation.
5. Prepared well in advance of suit or specific claim or threat of claim.
6. Routine claims investigations, reports, or evaluations prior to denial of claim.
7. Material is evidence in case.

Material prepared in anticipation of litigation may be obtainable if the following can be shown:

1. Substantial need for material in preparation of own case.
2. Unable to obtain it or substantial equivalent without undue hardship.
    a) Statements that contain fresh account right after event, and witness not available to party until memory gone.
    b) Witness reluctant or hostile; who has control is important.
    c) Witness may have had lapse of memory.
    d) Witness may be deviating from prior statement.
3. Witness may be able to obtain own statements given to party before trial.

In planning the discovery phase of your case, you should outline the elements required to establish (or rebut) a prima facie case for each theory of the case. List the basic facts that may support each element of a theory. Under each fact list the evidence that may help to prove the facts.

• What you have.
• What you *must* get.

- What you would *like* to have.
- How to prove or obtain proof—experts, witnesses, exhibits.

In developing a plan of discovery, consider the various discovery tools available to achieve the desired ends in light of the other factors of the case. It is also important to stay organized throughout discovery and not let anything slip through the cracks. Some kind of date/tickler system can be very helpful, such as the Office Memorandum of Form 6–7. The basic tools include the following—interrogatories, requests for documents, motions for medical examinations, notice of depositions, requests for admissions, and expert background.

I. Interrogatories—Federal Rule 33

This approach is best used early in litigation to obtain general information such as potential individuals to depose, subject matter warranting further inquiry, and documents you may wish to have produced. In other words, interrogatories lay the groundwork for other types of discovery.

Interrogatories are a simple and economical device for obtaining information. However, they are limited to parties. Moreover, responses are limited to questions asked, with no opportunity for immediate follow-up as would be possible in an oral deposition. Battling over inadequate answers can be a long, frustrating process. Another shortcoming of interrogatories is that the answers are drafted (and therefore carefully worded) by lawyers.

Use interrogatories to determine the following:

1. the factual and legal bases for the pleadings;
2. the appropriate person(s) from whom additional information may be obtained;
3. the names of individuals having knowledge of facts relating to the case and witnesses who may be called at trial (if expert witnesses— their backgrounds and what they will give as testimony);
4. the existence, coverage, and extent of insurance;
5. similar incidents relating to the subject matter of the case;
6. the existence and location of documents and tangible things;
7. business and corporate information;
8. financial information; and
9. the factual basis underlying any affirmative causes or defenses raised.

The serving party should keep a diary of answer deadlines for follow-up letters or motions to compel. Responding parties have a duty to investigate and must reveal information they or their agents know, believe, learned through hearsay, have in their records, or have in their possession, and control. If motions are pending, that may eliminate need for discovery on same issues. One or both parties may request postponement of discovery on those issues until the motions have been decided. Answers must be complete but may be qualified due to lack of information or other reasons. Reasons for such qualified answers must be given.

Objections to interrogatories may include:

1. information sought not relevant;
2. question too vague or broad;
3. privilege;
4. trial preparation material and no showing of substantial need and inability to obtain; and
5. unreasonably great burden on respondent.

The responding party must specify grounds for objection (what and why improper) in answers to specific interrogatories. File a motion for protective order if necessary.

In the event that a party has objected to or otherwise neglected or refused to respond to legitimate discovery requests, counsel are required under the federal rule and in many states to confer together in a good faith attempt to resolve any discovery dispute. Often a letter that describes the nature of the dispute and the reasons why a party considers a response incomplete or evasive together with citations to appropriate legal authorities can avoid litigation of discovery disputes. Counsel are urged to attempt to confer in good faith to resolve such disputes so as to avoid the delay and the costs associated with litigation of discovery. Motion to compel answers can be filed if answers cannot be obtained informally.

II. Production of Documents and Things— Federal Rule 34

This device is best used early in litigation before taking any depositions. Like responses to interrogatories, documents produced may reveal potential witnesses and subject matter warranting further inquiry. Consider using it in connection with interrogatories.

The request may be utilized to inspect, examine, test, copy, and photograph documents or objects in possession or control of another party. It is not limited to documents. Tangible things that can be inspected, copied, tested, or sampled may be produced. Real and personal property may be inspected, measured, surveyed, photographed, tested, and sampled.

You must describe the documents or things requested with reasonable accuracy so that the responding party easily can understand which materials must be produced. You must give a time, place, and manner for inspection and copying or provide that time, place, and manner will be mutually agreed upon by the parties at a later date.

Every motion should state grounds for production. Good cause grounds for requiring production are:

1. unavailability from other sources;
2. relevance to merits and necessary proofs;
3. no undue hardship on defendant to produce;
4. urgency or need of plaintiff; and
5. failure to produce would prejudice plaintiff's preparation or cause undue hardship or injustice.

The responding party may reply in one or more of the following ways:

1. make available the documents and things, requested;
2. serve written response permitting inspection and copying at another time or in another manner (when documents are too voluminous to be easily transmitted);
3. move for a protective order per Federal Rule 26(C); and
4. object, stating the reasons for the objection
    a. nonexistence of items
    b. noncontrol in respondent
    c. nonrelevance
    d. privilege
    e. trial preparation or informally retained expert
    f. burdensome, vague, or overbroad.

One of the most important, and potentially troublesome, aspects of document production is keeping track of what has been produced and received. Put sequential numbers (Bates Stamp) on all documents being produced. Keep a set of copies, a document production log (see Form 6–1), and a cover letter or motion response describing the documents and referencing the numbers. Carefully review all documents received from the other side. If they are numbered, create a similar log and a separate file copy set. If they are not numbered, consider numbering them yourself to minimize later problems.

III. Physical Examinations—Federal Rule 35

This motion permits mental, physical, or blood examination by a physician. The examining party should send a referral letter to the doctor briefly summarizing the accident or circumstances of the physical problem, major complaints, and questions to be answered by doctor, keeping in mind that the referral letter will be seen by opposing parties.

It is limited to actions in which the mental or physical condition or blood relationship of an individual is in controversy. Good cause must be shown for compulsory examinations. The prospective information must be relevant, and the moving party must need the information.

Examinations are limited to parties, agents of parties, or persons under control of parties.

Objection may be raised by motion for protective orders so as to:

- examination itself or scope of exam;
- refuse use of untried or dangerous medical procedure;
- prevent use of hypnotism, truth serum, or other questionable drugs or procedures as nonrelevant;
- require reasonable time and place;
- oppose doctor as incompetent or biased; and
- require presence of own doctor.

Plaintiff's preparation of client for defendant examination include the following:

1. Get defendant to examine plaintiff right away, particularly where objective signs are present.
2. Prepare client prior to examination.
   a. Review history; use records and reports.
   b. Doctor will observe ordinary actions—walking, sitting, bending to remove shoes, going up or down steps.
   c. Instruct client to voice complaints, feelings, and responses to tests
3. Set exam at time of day plaintiff feels worst.
4. Send hospital and doctor reports to examining doctor. Summarize injuries and complaints for doctor.
5. Examine all prosthetics or braces for wear.
6. Instruct client to note and remember time and circumstances of exam.
   a. length of wait in reception room.
   b. length of wait in exam room.

   c. length of time to get history.

   d. length of actual exam.

   e. questions asked and tests performed.

7. Have plaintiff examined by treating physician same day.

8. Obtain copy of doctor's report from examining party.

IV. Depositions—Federal Rules 27, 28, 29, 30, 31, and 32

Use responses to interrogatories and requests for production and all investigation materials in preparing for deposition. The notice of deposition should be sufficient to compel attendance of party deponents. A subpoena is necessary to compel nonparties. Always consider both a testimony subpoena *and* a subpoena duces tecum for production of documents at deposition.

Pretrial purposes of depositions are:

1. Perpetuation of trial testimony. Preserve testimony in case deponent is unable to testify later at trial.

2. Discovery.

   a. Obtain information with the advantage of being able to ask follow-up questions.

   b. Ask about everything. This is the time to learn facts that could sabotage your case. Do not wait until trial!

   c. Determine extent and limits of deponent's knowledge.

   d. Obtain admissions and authenticate documents.

   e. Force deponent to state a version of the facts under oath, thus obligating the deponent to stand by that version or be subject to impeachment and court sanctions. Fully develop inaccuracies, exaggerations, lies, and so on.

   f. Evaluate deponent's ability as a trial witness and potential impression on jury.

   g. Explore weaknesses on both sides of the action.

Trial use of depositions are:

1. Preservation of testimony of absent witnesses.

2. Impeachment of witness or party.

3. Admissions against interest by party.

4. Using part of deposition.

   a. If one side uses only a part of a deposition at trial, the other side may require other parts introduced.

    b. Considerations on using part.
       1) Do other portions contain innuendoes that are unfair or inaccurate but hard to rebut?
       2) Do other portions contain material damaging to other party so won't introduce?
       3) Is there any way to prove the point besides using portion of deposition?

Depositions are generally taken after interrogatories and motions to produce documents. Take depositions of hostile witnesses early to fix their testimony before they have been coached about the case. You may want to try to take all depositions of parties and hostile witnesses on the same day, if possible. Depositions are technically open to anyone who wants to attend—parties and other witnesses. If you are concerned about educating a hostile witness prior to his or her deposition, move for a protective order to exclude him or her from prior depositions.

Everything you have done previously feeds into the process of preparing for and taking depositions. This is your opportunity to really test your case—and theirs—and prepare for trial. Many cases rise or fall on the depositions: one side or the other decides that what looked bad in deposition will look worse at trial, and the case is settled. The Deposition Overview at Form 6–3 may help you think about how to construct your depositions. The three motor vehicle accident (MVA) case deposition checklists (obviously written somewhat from the plaintiff's side: Defendant's Deposition, Form 6–4; Plaintiff's Doctor, Form 6–5; and Defendant's Doctor, Form 6–6, should provide some further food for thought.

Trial preparation is all about connections: one thing leads to another. Yet those connections are often lost when things are just thrown in the file. Immediately after every deposition, you should prepare a short "exit memo" (see Form 6–2). The purposes of this memo include highlighting key testimony and documents, noting your personal impressions while they are still fresh, and compiling all new leads and ideas for follow-up.

V. Requests for Admissions—Federal Rule 36

This is technically an issue-narrowing device, rather than discovery, but it is used during the discovery phase of litigation. It is utilized to establish facts and legal issues and authenticate documents without having to prove them at trial. It further reduces time and expense of introducing evidence at trial.

Requests are deemed admitted unless there is a written answer or objection within an appropriate response period. Attorneys' fees and costs may be awarded where a party proves a fact that was denied without reasonable basis.

A request for admission is often used as a formal device for eliminating issues based on responses given to interrogatories or in depositions, but it can sometimes be helpful at the outset of litigation to eliminate much costly discovery. You may also be able to secure damaging admissions before your opponent can formulate a case strategy.

Possible responses to a request for admission include the following:

1. Admission.
2. Denial.
3. Statement of reasons for inability to admit or deny (see federal rules for procedure for neither admitting nor denying).
4. Objection.
5. Request for an extension of time to respond; leave of court may be required by local rules.

VI. Experts

If an expert is to be a witness, you may discover name, subject matter, facts, opinions, and grounds for opinion. It may be necessary to submit interrogatories regarding these matters before the expert's deposition may be taken. If expert is specially employed for the case but is not listed as a witness, there is no discovery of opinions except in exceptional circumstances making it impracticable for party to obtain own expert opinion, such as:

• test item is lost or destroyed.
• party cannot obtain own expert.

An in-house expert may or may not be exempt. A nonwitness expert who is consulted informally is generally considered nondiscoverable.

Further Reading

American Bar Association Section of Litigation. *The Litigation Manual.* (John G. Koeltl and John Kiernan, eds.) Chicago: American Bar Association, 1983.

Barthold, Walter. *Attorney's Guide to Effective Discovery Techniques.* Englewood Cliffs, NJ: Prentice-Hall, Inc., 1975.

Bender's Forms of Discovery. Vols. 1–16. New York: Matthew Bender, 1984.

Danner, Douglas. *Pattern Deposition Checklists.* The Lawyers Co-operative Publishing Co.; San Francisco: Bancroft-Whitney Co., 1984.

Deposition Strategy: Law and Forms. Vols. 1–10. New York: Matthew Bender, 1984.

Dombroff, Mark A. "Requests for Admissions: Weighing the Pros and Cons." *Trial* (June 1983): 82–85.

Haydock, Roger S., and David F. Herr. *Discovery Practice.* Boston: Little, Brown and Company, 1982.

Shephard's Discovery Proceedings in Federal Practice. Colorado Springs, CO: Shephard's/McGraw-Hill, 1983.

6-1 DOCUMENT PRODUCTION LOG

<u>Smith v. Jones</u>: Documents Produced to: _____

Production Number	Date of Production	Bates Numbers	Description	Confirming Witness
1.				
2.				
3.				
4.				
5.				

6-2 DEPOSITION EXIT MEMO

To:_____ Case File/ _____ Witness File

From: _____, Esq.

Re:_____ Deposition Dated: _____

1) Persons Present:

_____

_____

_____

2) Highlights
   Key testimony: _____

_____

_____

Observations: _____

_____

Key Exhibits: _____

_____

3) Follow-Up
   Documents _____

_____

Other Leads: _____

_____

Trial: _____

_____

4) Comments: _____

_____

Court reporter: _____ Phone number: _____

Transcript: _____ Requested _____ Obtained Date _____

__Transcript reviewed for errors __Corrected Reviewed/signed by witness date _____

Location of exhibits: _____

_____

6-3 DEPOSITION OVERVIEW—GENERAL

A. Preparation for deposition.

    1. Outline proof for prima facie case.
        a. List facts necessary to prove or counter each theory of case.
        b. Under each fact, list proof.
            1) What you have.
            2) What you must obtain.
            3) What you would like to have.
            4) How to prove or obtain proof—expert, witness, exhibit.

    2. Study background and subject before deposing expert.

B. Scope of deposition.

    1. General rule—limit exam.
        a. Limit scope to issues on which you need information.
        b. Limit scope to obtaining helpful testimony.
        c. Don't cover issues on which you have or can otherwise obtain the facts or on which information and questioning would disclose strengths, strategies, or weaknesses unknown to other party.
        d. The exception is a pure discovery deposition where you have very few facts or a hostile witness deposition where you want to commit witness to a specific set of facts.

    2. Specific areas that may be allowed.
        a. Reports of previous injury, accidents, incidents.
        b. Reports of subsequent injuries or accidents.
        c. Subsequent repairs or modifications.
        d. Opinions, factual conclusions, contentions.
        e. Expert's opinions and reports.
        f. Matters relating to damages.
        g. Eyewitnesses and statements.

    3. Purposes in deposing adverse party.
        a. Discovery, admissions, impeachment, to prepare plaintiff.
        b. Plan cross-exam.
        c. Develop settlement.
        d. Don't take when you may not want your party or other witness deposed.

C. Method of examination.

1. Discovery—use broad, open-ended questions.

2. Perpetuation—question as at trial.

3. Questioning technique.
    a. Avoid negative questions.
    b. Don't suggest answer in question unless you are leading for a reason.
    c. Avoid compound questions.
    d. Follow-up on answers.
    e. Insist on responsive answers.
        1) Demand accuracy.
        2) Establish time, distance, by reference points.
    f. Describe nonvocal gestures for the record.

4. Hostile witness or party.
    a. Counteract preparation by skipping around in beginning.
    b. Prepare questions designed to elicit admissions.
    c. Commit to details of admissions or contradictory statements.
    d. Establish admissions with orderly consolidation of prior admissions at end.
    e. Save impeaching questions for trial.
    f. Do not educate by nature or substance of questions.
    g. Do not educate by off-the-record discussions.
    h. Lead an exaggerating witness into further exaggeration.
    i. Commit a lying witness to details and circumstances.

5. When you obtain testimony helpful to you or harmful to adversary:
    a. Close any loopholes or avenues of escape.
    b. Do not warn adversary by repeating questions.

6. Authenticate exhibits.

7. Prepare for future use of part of deposition.
    a. Prevent attempts to include damaging material by opponent.
    b. Introduce material damaging to other side in client's deposition.

D. Improbability, inconsistency, and error

1. Improbability—inherent illogic
    a. Get to admit each link in logical chain of facts.
    b. Pin down to all details to foreclose future explanation.

2. Improbability—faulty observation or recollection.
    a. Suddenness of events and time in which happened.

    b. Minuteness of time in which any detail occurred.

    c. Number of things happening at time to confuse perception.

    d. Time when witness first tried to put all impressions into whole.

    e. Distinguish recollection from judgment, assumptions, or conjecture.

3. Conduct inconsistent with validity or belief in claim. Establish all instances of such conduct.

4. Error in fact or basis for assumptions. Commit witness to facts or basis by reiterating.

E. Objections—during deposition; at trial.

1. Deposition taken subject to "usual stipulations."
    a. That notary has directed witness to answer questions.
    b. That all objections reserved except as to form.
    c. That if witness doesn't sign after opportunity, used as signed.
       1) Waiver of exam and reading by parties and witness.
       2) Waiver of signing by witness.
       3) If not waived, cannot be used at trial unless witness has opportunity to read and sign.

2. Objections to form.
    a. Errors that can be corrected immediately may be waived unless made on record.
       1) In manner of taking deposition.
       2) In form of question or answer.
          a) Argumentative.
          b) Ambiguous.
          c) Compound or confusing questions.
       3) In oath or affirmation.
       4) In conduct of parties.
    b. Objections to value of evidence—not waived unless could be cured immediately.
       1) Reserve objections to competency for trial unless answer would be both excludable and unfairly prejudicial or privileged.
       2) Refusal to answer.
          a) Ask all questions in objectionable line for record.
          b) Finish deposition on unobjectionable matters.
          c) Obtain court ruling on all unanswered questions.
       3) Objection to own question may be allowed, if opponent tries to introduce at trial.

6-4 DEPOSITION CHECKLIST—MVA CASE: DEFENDANT'S DEPOSITION

A. Personal History.
    ____ Name, address, birth date, Soc. Sec. #.
    ____ Spouse and date married.
    ____ Children's names and ages.
    ____ Education.
    ____ Employment (names, addresses, dates, and duties).
    ____ Criminal record.
    ____ Driving record.
        ___Accidents.
        ___Violations.
        ___License suspension.
    ____ Medical history.
        ___Glasses.
        ___Medication.
    ____ Prior claims and lawsuits.
    ____ Other.

B. Description of Accident.
    ____ Identity of parties and insurers.
    ____ Occupants of vehicle.
    ____ Description and mechanical condition of vehicle.
    ____ Prior activity.
        ___ Started out from (time and place).
        ___ Reason.
        ___ Activity before driving.
        ___ Route.
    ____ Weather conditions.
    ____ Description of area.
        ___ Streets—direction, lanes.
        ___ Traffic controls, signs.
        ___ Lighting and obstructions.
        ___ Familiarity.
    ____ How accident happened.
        ___ Location and direction of vehicles.
        ___ Distance when first saw plaintiff's car.
        ___ Speed at all times.
        ___ Movement of vehicles.
        ___ Actions and signals by drivers.
        ___ Attempts to avoid accident.

___ Brakes first applied.

___ Skid marks and debris.

___ Point of impact.

___ Vehicles.

___ Street.

___ Distance traveled after impact.

___ Location after accident.

___ Driving distractions.

____ Diagram scene.

____ Statements—parties, witness.

____ Photographs.

____ Witnesses.

____ Other.

C. Traffic ticket—trial or plea.

____ Plaintiff's negligence—basis for counterclaim, if any.

____ Joint enterprise.

____ Arrangements.

____ Benefit.

____ Control.

____ Permissive use.

____ Circumstances and limitations.

____ Scope of employment.

____ Other.

D. Condition of parties at scene.

____ First aid at scene.

____ How parties left scene.

____ Vehicle repaired.

____ By whom.

____ Estimates.

____ Medical (doctors and hospitals).

____ Other.

6-5 DEPOSITION CHECKLIST—MVA CASE: PLAINTIFF'S DOCTOR

A. Background Qualifications.
    ____ Length of time practiced specialty and so certified.
    ____ Professional honors attained.
    ____ Publications.
    ____ Medical or professional associations.
    ____ Teaching positions.
    ____ Hospitals associated with.
    ____ Courts qualified in before.

B. Case History.
    ____ Source (plaintiff or other).

C. Examination.
    ____ Type of exam (explain).
    ____ Report subjective complaints and explain.
    ____ Explain that it is essential to consider subjective complaints.
    ____ Objective findings, and explain significance.
    ____ Describe tests performed and explain.
       ___ If positive, explain significance.
    ____ X-rays—explain negative X-rays in soft-tissue injuries.
    ____ Other.

D. Diagnosis.
    ____ Initial diagnosis—definite or tentative.
       ___ If tentative, explain when reached definite diagnosis.
    ____ Number of similar cases, operations, X-rays, handled by doctor.
    ____ Other.

E. Treatment.
    ____ Course of treatment.
       ___ Narrate step by step.
    ____ Hospital records.
       ___ Narrate details step by step.
    ____ Other.

F. Prognosis.
    ____ Relate to most recent findings, history, and present complaints.
    ____ Disability.
       ___ Limitations on everyday life.

___ Limitations on work ability.
___ How produced by injury.
___ Define disability.
___ How long lasted or will last.
___ Future or prolonged effect of continued medications.
___ Permanency.
___ Future medical treatments or operations.
___ Other.

G. Causation.
___ Prepare hypothetical question or lay foundation for opinion questions by establishing basis for opinions.
___ Opinion on causation to reasonable medical certainty or probability.
___ Reasons for opinion—how arrived at conclusions.

H. Medical Expenses.
___ How long in hospital?
___ How many visits to doctor?
___ Over how long a period of time?
___ Hospital bill—necessary as result of injury; customary and reasonable charges for community.
___ Doctor bill—necessary as result of injury; customary and reasonable charges for community.
___ Reasonable and probable future medical expenses.
___ Other.

6-6 DEPOSITION CHECKLIST—MVA CASE: DEFENDANT'S DOCTOR

A. Qualifications.
____ Education.
____ Specialty and board certification.
___ Testifying outside of specialty?
___ Books, articles, authored by doctor.
____ Resources that doctor considers authoritative.
____ Type and number of patients in same category as plaintiff.
____ Other.

B. Financial bias.
____ Charge per exam, report, pretrial conference, court appearance.
____ Number of times in last year made exams on plaintiff's or defendant's clients and number of times testified in court.
___ Establish by starting with number of times per day and multiply.
____ Number of times did same for opposite side.

C. Exam and treatment.
____ Limit to notes and records rather than recollection.
___ Get to admit has no independent recollection of exam because sees so many patients over the years.
____ Use notes and reports to limit testimony and evasiveness.
____ Cooperation and honesty of plaintiff.
___ Foundation—doctor can tell malingerer by experience.
___ Responses to tests were consistent with claims.
___ Admit plaintiff not malingerer.
____ Function of injured joint or area—foundation for future complications.
____ Admissions.
___ Not treating doctor, examined plaintiff once, only for purpose of report to defendant's insurance company and for testifying.
___ Does not know plaintiff as well as treating doctor, and plaintiff's doctor in better position to give complete picture of extent and nature of injury.
___ Treatment by plaintiff's doctor proper for type of injury diagnosed.
___ Concede plaintiff's doctor's qualifications.
___ Difference in opinion between doctors not unusual, and cannot say with certainty that plaintiff's doctor was wrong.
____ Subjective complaints.
___ Cannot say plaintiff does not feel pain—only cannot find objective signs.

___ Concede he treats his own patients on basis of subjective complaints without objective signs.

___ Tenderness is significant sign of nonvisible injury or underlying condition or pathology.

___ Review complaints of pain in history and exam by plaintiff's doctor.

___ Review complaints of pain at time of his exam—consistent.

___ Plaintiff's subjective complaints of pain in certain body areas consistent with plaintiff's evidence.

___ If assume truth and accuracy of complaints, must agree with plaintiff's doctor's diagnosis.

____ Recovery marked by periods of remission and exacerbation—no way of knowing if during exam plaintiff was having a "good" or "bad" day.

____ Doctor did not determine whether plaintiff had taken drugs or muscle relaxants prior to exam; what effect they could have on a plaintiff's responses; could mask symptoms.

____ Negative X-rays—does not preclude soft-tissue injury and other condition.

___ Supporting muscles, tissues, ligaments, not shown on X-ray.

____ Method of exam—faulty or incomplete.

___ One exam not as good as series of exams.

___ After one exam, forms tentative diagnosis and occasionally later decides it's wrong.

____ Causation.

___ Admit doctor has no idea of severity of trauma.

___ No knowledge of damage to car, speed.

___ Type of accident capable of causing injuries treated.

___ Accident only cause shown for whatever symptoms of injury in defendant's doctor's history and findings.

____ Prognosis.

___ Concede doctor has little knowledge of plaintiff's specific work duties or leisure activities.

___ Disability opinion based on this knowledge.

___ Admit acute condition may become chronic.

____ Defense of preexisting arthritis.

___ Admit arthritis present in most over-forty-years-old and frequently causes pain or disability.

___ Makes affected person more prone to injury and delays healing process.

____ Re-emphasize plaintiff's case by sticking to accepted medical propositions of plaintiff's injury—muscle spasm characteristics and meaning.

6-7 OFFICE MEMORANDUM RELATIVE TO CLIENT'S DISCOVERY PROCEDURES

Case No. _____, Circuit Court of _____County, Illinois.
_____, Plaintiff vs._____, et al., Defendants

Opponents			
Demand to Produce Served			
Compliance with Demand to Produce Due/Rec'd			
Mot. to Compel Production Filed			
Ord. Compelling Production Entered			
Interr. Served			
Obj. to Interr. Due/Rec'd			
Ans. to Interr. Due/Rec'd			
Mot. to Compel Ans. to Interr. Filed			
Ord. to Ans. Interr. Entered			
Not of Disc. Dep. Served			
Dates of Depo.			
Ct. Rpt. Trans of Dep. Rec'd			
Abst. of Depo. Made			

Opponent's Names / Lawyers(s) for Defendant:_____
_____
_____

7 | Motion Practice

Many cases are won or lost long before trial, through skillful motion practice. Pretrial pleadings can do everything from resolving discovery disputes to resolving the case. You should carefully and creatively consider what motions would be helpful and appropriate at every step of the way. The names and types of motions vary widely depending on the type of case, the jurisdiction, and other factors. However, it is worth discussing the most common general categories. Rules covering pleadings vary widely among different jurisdictions and courts. Consult all applicable rules before proceeding. For reference purposes here, we will cite some of the Federal Rules of Civil Procedure on point.

I. Initial Pleadings

Complaint

A civil case generally begins with the filing and service of a Complaint. Various aspects of the drafting, filing, and service of a Complaint are covered in Rules 3–11, Fed. R. Civ. Proc. At or around the time the Complaint is filed, a plaintiff can also file a variety of other pleadings, including the following.

Prejudgment Security

A great jury verdict doesn't mean much if you cannot collect the money. If there is good reason—and evidentiary grounds—for concern, you might want to consider asking for some form of prejudgment security against property, bank accounts, wages, or whatever. Federal Rule 64 lists some of the more common remedies as "arrest, attachment, garnishment, replevin, sequestration, and other . . ." The Notes of the Rule list many of the specific federal statutes.

Injunctions

Sometimes the relief that is needed, either in the short term or the long term, is not just financial but requires some action (or inaction) by the parties. In such a case, you should consider seeking immediate injunctive relief. Indeed, some types of cases are often effectively won or lost at the early injunction stage (employee noncompetes, certain antitrust cases, and so forth). Federal Rule 64 sets out of some of the process and standards for obtaining a Temporary Restraining Order, Preliminary Injunction, and Permanent Injunction.

II. Responsive Pleadings

Answer

Too many lawyers treat the Answer to a Complaint as a mere formality. However, there are both strategic and legal reasons for taking it much more seriously. Strategically, it is an early opportunity to work closely with your client in reviewing the case, to carefully consider its strengths and weaknesses, and to present a solid and convincing response to the other side. Legally, an inadequate Answer can waive denials or defenses, and an inaccurate Answer can cause a variety of problems down the line. Federal Rules 8, 12, and 13 provide guidance on the Answer and Counterclaims.

Motions

Certain defenses can or must be made by motion, along with or even before an Answer. Federal Rule 12 lists some of the grounds for motions:

12(b): (1) lack of jurisdiction over the subject matter, (2) lack of jurisdiction over the person, (3) improper venue, (4) insufficiency of process, (5) insufficiency of service of process, (6) failure to state a claim upon which   relief can be granted, (7) failure to join a party under Rule 19;

12(e): Motion for More Definite Statement;

12(f): Motion to Strike.

III. Discovery

Many courts have tried hard to minimize discovery motion practice by requiring automatic discovery, meetings, cooperative efforts to resolve disputes, and other guidelines. See, for example, Federal Rules 26 and 37. If that is not adequate, motion practice can take various forms.

Motion to Compel

If you are unable to resolve a discovery dispute, and the discovery you seek is important to you, you may wish to file a Motion to Compel, as under Federal Rule 37.

Protective Order / Motion to Quash

If the other side is seeking discovery that is irrelevant, privileged, burdensome, or otherwise improper, you can ask the court to limit discovery. See for example, Federal Rule 30.

IV. Dispositive

As the facts of a case are filled out through discovery, or as the legal issues become clear, many cases are resolved without trial, through dispositive motions. Even if the judge does not grant the relief, a well-crafted motion and memorandum can go a long way towards to the demonstrating other side—and sometimes to the court—the problems with their case.

Judgment on the Pleadings

This motion, as described in Federal Rule 12(c), is sometimes used as a middle ground between a 12(b)6 Motion to Dismiss and the more extensive process of Summary Judgment.

Summary Judgment

This most common form of dispositive motion allows the judge to rule on all or part of the case without a trial if, based on the discovery and affidavits filed with the motion, "there is no genuine issue as to any material fact and the moving party is entitled to a judgment as a matter of law." Federal Rule 56.

V. Evidentiary

While most evidentiary issues are resolved by objections at trial, there are often times when important issues can and should be resolved pretrial. Here again, even if the court decides to defer a decision until trial, an effective pleading can help educate the judge on the case and on the particular issue and evidence. These pleadings are generally in the form of the Motions in Limine (from the Latin, "at the threshold," "at the beginning") asking the court to make certain evidentiary rulings pretrial (in a criminal case, this may also be in the form of a Motion to Suppress).

VI. Trial Memo / Brief

Before any trial, you should consider filing a trial brief or memo outlining your case and the issues presented at trial. Check your local rules: in some courts a trial brief, or even a joint trial memorandum, is required. However, even when it is not required, a trial brief can be a good opportunity to help educate the judge before trial, and give the judge a reference document during trial.

Forms in Chapter 8

8 | Settlement

ost cases should, and do, settle. However, taking any settlement for granted puts you and your client at a great disadvantage. One of the most fundamental requirements for successful negotiation in any field is the ability to communicate your willingness to walk away from the table. In litigation, this translates into convincing the other side—through hard work, not just rhetoric—that you are ready, willing, and able to go to trial. Indeed, it has often been said that the best way to avoid going to trial is to be ready to go to trial.

Not only do you have to be prepared for trial, you must also be prepared for settlement. Effective settlement negotiations and outcomes require careful analysis and preparation. That includes analysis of your case, your client, your judge and local juries, opposing counsel, and the opposing party or parties. Only then can you begin to negotiate.

I. Types of Settlement

Traditional Lump Sum

The most common type of settlement remains the simple exchange of cash payment for dismissal and release. In many cases this is the most appropriate—and often the only appropriate—result. The challenge comes in evaluating the right amount (see below).

Structured Settlement

A structured settlement is usually a combination of up-front cash at settlement (often at the client's request) and a series of future payments to the plaintiff. The up-front cash may be allocated to the plaintiff, incurred medical expenses, rehabilitation costs, attorney fees, and any other expenses requiring immediate payment. The series of payments are designed to meet the needs of the plaintiff. Future medical costs, educational funds, lost wage income, and rehabilitative costs can be provided by using a combination of monthly payments and single-sum amounts at specified future dates.

A structured settlement can also help account for inflation by providing an annual increase factor (such as 3 percent, 4 percent) to the monthly payments and a series of periodic lump-sum payments. For example, a settlement paying $1,000 per month and guaranteed for 30 years, would afford a total payout of $360,000. If an annual inflation factor of just 3 percent was added to the same $1,000 per month, the total payout would be increased to $570,905. The inflation factor in conjunction with the lump-sums should provide adequate protection for the plaintiff.

The principal pros and cons of structured settlements include the following (see Further Reading list for more detail):

Pros

- structured security for many clients, including the younger or less sophisticated, to avoid either dissipation of a lump-sum or the costs and risks of managing investments;
- tax advantages (see materials and IRS Code);
- flexibility in design, to structure for particular client's needs;
- the up-front cost (and appearance) may be lower for the defendant and more attractive as a means of getting to an agreement.

Cons

- there may be good reasons why a client, particularly a more financially sophisticated one, wants money up-front;
- the flexibility in negotiation ends once the structure is created and does not allow for changes to address a client's changed needs (other than the rapidly evolving "gray market" for purchasing structured settlements at a hefty discount);
- the tax advantages may be relatively small, depending on the tax bracket;
- since structured settlements are often done through separate insurance or annuity companies, there is some added risk if that company should fail.

Other Relief

Sometimes some—or even all—of the relief sought is not financial. The range of other considerations is enormous, but may include issues of employment, housing, noncompetition, real estate boundaries or conditions, transactions or other business considerations, nondisparagement, and much more. However, the further away the deal gets from simple cash, the more difficult it may be to set the agreement out clearly and provide for enforcement, disputes, and protection down the line.

II. Evaluation

Consider the following basic factors in the cases:

- Liability.
- Injury/damage.
- Client characteristics.
- Defendant's characteristics.
- Liquidated damages.
- Cost of litigation—client and defendant.
- Prior judgment values.

The main objective at this stage is to identify the strengths and weaknesses of both your case and your opponent's on the basis of these factors. By weighing these strengths and weaknesses, you will make your evaluation of the case for settlement purposes. Although for convenience much of this is described from the plaintiff's perspective, the same process should be undertaken by defense counsel.

Liability

Determine the probability of a verdict in your client's favor by applying the applicable law to the facts. Identify the facts necessary to establish a prima facie case together with the defenses available, including any affirmative defenses. List each issue in your case and the facts required to support the issue. Next, note all of these facts that can be proven in your client's case. Finally, opposite each issue, list those facts available in defense of the issue. Admissible evidence is the key factor in this determination.

Injury/Damage

Determine all elements of the client's injury or loss that may be recovered and what proof is required. Look for any unusual nature of the loss that may influence an award, such as severity, permanency, disfigurement, or other inflammatory elements. Consider factors that may either give rise to punitive damages or influence the award, such as gross or wanton negligence, intentional acts, or target defendant status. Actual losses are more easily proved and acceptable to jurors than losses that are speculative or difficult to conceptualize. Losses that can be described through demonstrative evidence as well as testimony may be more easily recovered than losses only describable by testimony, particularly in complex business or technical issue cases.

Special Damages

These are the out-of-pocket expenses incurred in the past or certain to occur in the future. Generally, these damages are not discounted in settlement except where the liability problems are such that you are only trying to cut your client's losses. In some cases, the special damages may be so large that they can affect the outcome of the case and award. Unusually high medical expenses lend support to the seriousness of the injury. Nominal special damages may have the reverse effect when you are seeking an unusually high general damage award. A sample worksheet to track damages is enclosed as Form 8–2.

Client Characteristics

Appraise the client's personality, age, sex, social and financial position in relation to the potential jurors. In personal injury cases, a disabling injury to a young male wage earner will be judged differently than the same injury to an elderly widow. Young children and elderly persons often receive less for nondisabling injuries than the middle-aged victim. The client's and witnesses' personalities and personal appearances may be the most important factors in determining the outcome and size of the verdict in the close case.

Opposing Party's Characteristics

The same factors that apply to the client apply to the opposing party. In addition, the two most important characteristics of the defendant are position of leverage in relation to the plaintiff and financial ability to respond in damages. The outcome of the case and size of award may depend upon whether the defendant had a better opportunity than the plaintiff to avoid or prevent the loss or whether the defendant's position vis-à-vis the plaintiff's caused a situation in which plaintiff incurred a loss. The existence of a "deep pocket" defendant, such as an insurance company or large corporation, will favorably affect the case value, while an individual defendant's inability to pay a judgment will adversely affect the settlement value.

Costs of Litigation

1. <u>Financial costs.</u> The expected litigation costs for each side are obviously a factor to be considered in relation to the probability of obtaining a favorable verdict and the expected size of the verdict.
2. <u>Emotional costs.</u> Consider the emotional impact of a trial on the parties, including such factors as opposing counsel's style, whether a party will be accused of wrongdoing or lying, personal matters that will be aired publicly, and unpleasant events that must be relived at trial.

Prior Judgment Values

Prior awards are one yardstick for evaluating a settlement offer. They are the only guide by which lawyers can predict the future. However, they should be used only as a guide and not as a limit, since no two cases or juries are exactly the same. There are loose-leaf services that offer information, organized by jurisdiction, for evaluating personal injury cases based on past verdicts (see Further Reading list).

Settlement Formulas

Some lawyers have developed settlement formulas for evaluating a case based on these and other factors. These formulas will assign a numerical weight to each factor determined to be important. The total of the weighted-factor values is a percentage figure that is multiplied by the ideal or average judgment value to arrive at the settlement value. All approaches to settlement evaluation are based on a cost/benefit-versus-risk evaluation. Consider the costs to the client, both in monetary and emotional expense, of proceeding to trial against the probability of winning and the net return that can be expected.

III. Offer and Negotiation

Once evaluation is complete, make an offer based on the strength of your case and/or the weakness of your opponent's case.

Discuss your evaluation with your client and obtain settlement authority. Confirm evaluation and authority in writing with most clients. The timing of the offer will depend upon the size and complexity of your case. In a case involving minor, nondisabling injuries with short-term treatment, the offer may be made after "maximum medical cure" and negotiated with an insurance adjuster without filing suit. Where your case has some undiscovered (by the other side) weaknesses, settlement before suit and discovery may be advisable.

Cases involving major and complex losses or long-term treatment or requiring discovery of information in defendant's possession should be settled only after filing suit and, in such instances, suit should be filed as soon as possible.

In determining the amount of your settlement demand, it is useful to familiarize yourself with reported jury awards or settlements reported in comparable cases within the jurisdiction where your case arose. Including awards from other cases involving comparable facts and injuries will strengthen the credibility of your written demand, as well as provide the practitioner with a reasonable basis for evaluating and responding to any response to the offer of settlement or counter offer. An offer of settlement that lacks sufficient basis cannot succeed. Additionally, it must be remembered that the practitioner has an obligation to report any offer of settlement to the client. By communicating settlement offers to the client and discussing the strengths and weaknesses in detail, the practitioner is not only discharging important ethical obligations but minimizing the chances of misunderstanding or disagreement with the client at a future time.

The offer may be instituted through either the settlement letter or settlement brochure (sample enclosed as Form 8–3 or 8–4). A written offer is preferable to an oral offer. The written offer not only documents your reasons for settlement to the local adjuster but also ensures that the home office claims supervisor will have your version of the offer and not that of an intermediary. Include in the offer the strengths you have identified in your case and the weaknesses in the opponent's case. Acknowledge and explain any weaknesses in your case that are known to the other side. Follow the offer with a settlement conference for further negotiation. The face-to-face settlement conference is preferable to the telephone negotiation in all but the most common or simple type cases. Doing your homework and presenting a solidly based offer is often the key to succession in that negotiation.

IV. The Lawyer's Role and Risks

Although a settlement offer should be based on the relative merits of the case and damages, any offer must be entirely the client's decision. Both the law in many states and common sense make clear that this is the client's absolute right. Some states make it risky for a lawyer to even make a recommendation. The reasons for this include:

- This is the client's case and the client's rights to legal process. The decision to settle is a decision to give up the case and those rights. A lawyer can help explain the pros and cons, but should not make the decision.

- It has often been said that a good compromise is when everyone walks away a little bit unhappy. You can help your client by lowering expectations and by anticipating and explaining this reality. However, you do not want that unhappiness directed at you for pushing too hard for a particular result.

- Hindsight is rarely 20/20, rather, it is often colored by intervening events and knowledge. In the period of let-down following a settlement, what seemed like a lot of money may disappear surprisingly quickly, the client may read or hear distorted accounts of the results in other cases (which are presumably newsworthy precisely because they are unusual or bizarre); there will be lots of people offering their advice after the fact that you settled for "too little." You want the record to be clear that the settlement was the client's decision: freely, voluntarily, and knowingly.

Help your client to understand the process, lay out the pros and cons, answer questions, but let the client decide.

V. ADR

No discussion of litigation, and particularly the likelihood of settlement, would be complete without referencing the growing popularity of Alternative Dispute Resolution (ADR). Although the variations are endless, the two basic forms of ADR in litigation matters are arbitration and mediation.

Arbitration

Arbitration involves submitting the dispute to an independent, generally private, arbitrator (or panel of arbitrators) for resolution outside of a formal court trial. Arbitration is generally determined *before* the dispute arises, generally because the contract or agreement between the parties contains an arbitration clause. However, once a dispute arises, arbitration can still be an option by agreement, providing all parties with a faster, less expensive, and possibly less adversarial or disruptive means of resolving the dispute. However, there are many cases where one or more parties want the full benefits of formal litigation and a jury verdict.

Mediation

Mediation generally involves bringing the parties and counsel in a dispute together with an outside mediator to attempt to resolve the case by negotiation and agreement. An increasing number of jurisdiction provide, encourage, or even require mediation before certain cases go to trial. Mediation can, in fact, be very helpful in resolving a case by bringing the parties together and forcing an early evaluation of the case, and the costs and risks of trial.

Further Reading

Baer, Harold, and Aaron J. Broder. *How To Prepare and Negotiate Cases for Settlement.* New York: Law-Arts Publishers, 1973.

Danninger, Johnson, and Lesti. "Structured Settlements: A Negotiating Guide." 15 *Trial Law. Q.* 30 (1983).

Hornwood, Sanford W., and I. Lucretia Hollingsworth. *Systematic Settlements: Second Edition.* Rochester, NY: Lawyers Co-operative Publishing Co.

Kligler, Richard I. *Structured Settlements as a Negotiating Tool.* New York: Practicing Law Institute, 1992.

Lesti, Paul J., Brent B. Daninger, and Robert N. Johnson. *Structured Settlements.* Rochester, NY; Lawyers Co-operative Publishing Co.

Miller, Henry G. *Art of Advocacy—Settlements.* New York: Matthew Bender and Co.

Simmons, Robert L. *Wining Before Trial: How to Prepare Cases for the Best Settlement or Trial Result.* Englewood Cliffs, NJ: Executive Reports Corp.

Sperber, Philip. *Attorney's Guide to Negotiations.* Wilmette, Ill.: Callaghan & Co.

Werchick, Arne. "Settling the Case—Plaintiff." 4 *Am. Jur. Trials.*

Yandell, Dirk. "Advantages and Disadvantages of Structured Settlements." *Journal of Legal Economics* 1995.

8-1 SETTLEMENT CHECKLIST

A. Investigation and research.

    1. Obtain all facts.

    2. Analyze facts and identify issues.

    3. Research law on issues.

    4. Reinvestigate for additional facts or clarification.

    5. Reanalyze and narrow issues.

B. Evaluation.

    1. Liability.
       a. List facts required for prima facie case.
       b. List known facts in case to prove prima facie case.
       c. List available defenses and known facts to support.
       d. Identify strengths and weaknesses of case and defense.
       e. Determine probability of verdict in client's favor.

    2. Injury/damage. Identify all recoverable items of damage or loss.
       a. Pain and suffering.
          1) Physical and mental—per day.
          2) Severe or inflammatory injury.
          3) Permanent disability.
          4) Psychological or nonapparent injury; such as, loss of enjoyment of life—whole-man theory.
       b. Future loss of wages, fringe benefits, profits.
          1) Past earning/profit history—tax returns, business records, fringe benefit plans.
          2) Economist or trade expert.
             a) Life-expectancy tables.
             b) Cost-of-living index, business and trade abstracts.
             c) Present value discount and inflation tables.
             d) Tax tables.

    3. Special damages.
       a. Medical—doctor, hospital, therapy, nursing, prosthetic devices, laboratory, and X-rays.
       b. Repair bills.
       c Loss of past earnings/profits.

       d.   Transportation.

       e.   Other out-of-pocket expenses.

4. Client characteristics.
   a. Personality and appearance.
   b. Age.
   c. Sex.
   d. Social and financial position in community.

5. Opposing party characteristics.
   a. Financial position in relation to plaintiff.
   b. Ability to control plaintiff or situation.
   c. Financial ability to respond in damages.
   d. Personality and personal appearance.
   e. Insurance limits.

6. Costs of litigation—financial and emotional.
   a. Plaintiff's estimated costs to prepare and try case.
   b. Defendant's estimated costs.
   c. Emotional costs to plaintiff and defendant.

7. Prior judgment values. Research reported verdicts and settlements in comparable cases. Determine high, low, and median judgments.

8. Evaluate.
   a. Settlement formulas.
   b. Increase or reduce judgment value by weight of other factors.
   c. Obtain settlement approval from client.

C. Offer and negotiation.

1. Timing of offer.
   a. Before suit.
      1) Small value, common facts and law situation, short-term injuries or damages.
      2) Offer and negotiate with adjuster.
   b. After suit and trial preparation.
      1) Large value, complex issues, long-term injury or loss.
      2) Offer and negotiate with attorney.

2. Manner of offer.
   a. Settlement letter.
   b. Settlement brochure, which should include the following:
      1) Personal records—birth, marriage, honors, military service.
      2) Death certificate or autopsy.

3) Accident reports, newspaper accounts.

4) Tables—life and work expectancy, interest.

5) Statement of facts.

6) Legal memoranda.

7) Witness statements.

8) Photographs—accident site, injuries, other subject matter.

9) Diagrams, charts, sketches.

10) Damages itemized in detail with documentation.

3. Amount of offer.
   a. Add additional amount (25 percent) to settlement value.
   b. Insurance policy limits where company liable for excess for failure to settle.
      1) Where individual defendant unable to respond in damages.
      2) Where multiple insurers can make settlement value.
      3) No serious question of liability.

4. Negotiation.

8-2 SETTLEMENT WORKSHEET

Special Damages

Item	Bill Received or Verified	Amount
Hospital _____	_____	_____
Hospital _____	_____	_____
Emergency_____	_____	_____
Dr. _____	_____	_____
Dr. _____	_____	_____
X-rays _____	_____	_____
X-rays _____	_____	_____
Dental _____	_____	_____
Physiotherapy _____	_____	_____
Drugs_____	_____	_____
Appliances _____	_____	
Ambulance _____	_____	_____
Total Medical		$_____
Wages _____	_____	_____
Domestic Help _____	_____	_____
Yard Help_____	_____	_____
Transportation _____	_____	_____
Personal property _____	_____	_____
Property damage (auto) _____	_____	_____
Others _____	_____	_____
Total Other		$_____
Grand Total		$_____

General Damages

Past pain and suffering, mental anguish, and so on.	_____
Future pain and suffering, mental anguish, and so on.	_____
Permanent disability, loss of enjoyment of life.	_____
Permanent disfigurement, embarrassment, and so on.	_____
Total General Damages	$_____

Case Expenses

Filing fees _____   Photos _____   Maps _____

Doctor's reports _____   Investigation _____   Travel _____

Depositions _____   Phone Calls _____   Photocopies _____

Total Case Expenses $_____

Settlement Negotiations

Date _____   Offer _____   Demand _____   To Do _____

Date _____   Offer _____   Demand _____   To Do _____

Date _____   Offer _____   Demand _____   To Do _____

8-3 SETTLEMENT LETTER WITH BROCHURE

September 1, 19/20__

Mr./Ms.
Attorney at Law
Baton Rouge, Louisiana 70821

Re: _____ v. _____

Dear _____:

I am enclosing a duplicate copy of settlement brochure materials for your clients so they may make their evaluation of this case.

Some thoughts on value while reviewing this file. First, Dr. Moroney, head of the school of economics, Tulane University, has taken all these facts and reached what he considers a reasonable and <u>conservative</u> appraisal of lost earning capacity of $395.736. Dr. Moroney is a highly qualified and experienced economist who spent a great deal of time studying the financial situation and the wage, price, and discount trends.

This is the only way to determine the value of a man's life—by logical and expert appraisal. To attempt to determine the survivor's compensation by an individual judge's estimation and intuition to this day and time is grossly archaic and unfair. Should we determine the value of a man's life in any less expert manner than we determine the value of appropriated land?

I have had to follow the "line of cases" approach in prior cases because the liability was a questionable factor, but this case would provide an excellent vehicle to change this approach.

Secondly, even using similar cases as a <u>low</u> guideline for settlement, Mrs. _____'s loss would be substantially close to the expert's evaluation.

In *Habert v. Patterson Truck Lines*, 247 Do. 2d 886, 3d (1971), writ. don. 249 So. 2d 209, concerning a 22-year-old decedent earning $3,795.97 per year, with 40.85-year life expectancy, the award was as follows:

Widow:	
Loss of support	$80,000
Love and affection	15,000
Daughter (2 1/2 months old:)	
Loss of support	25,000
Love and affection	9,000
	$129,000

In comparison, _____'s earnings can be conservatively figured at three to four times Habert, and his life expectancy is longer.

In *Allen v. Louisiana Power and Light Co.* 202 So. 2d 704, 3d (1967), writ ref. 204 So. 2d 574, concerning a 21-year-old decedent earning $4,800 per year with a 48-year life expectancy, the award was as follows:

Widow	$85,000
Daughter (2 years old)	45,000
	$130,000

Once again, _____'s earnings are three to four times as great and his life expectancy longer. Remember also that this is 1967 case, that verdicts generally increase 13.6 percent per year (see *Jury Verdict Research Series*), and that there has been a particularly sharp rise in earnings and inflation between 1968 and 1972.

In *Fairbanks v. Travelers Ins. Co.*, 232 So. 2d 323, 2d (1970), writ ref. 234 So. 2d 194, concerning 41- and 46-year old decedents earning $5,000 per year with expert estimates of future earnings of $65,000 to $168,000, the widows are awarded $89,333.

In comparison, _____'s earnings and life expectancy would be at least double, and there are no children in Fairbanks.

In Tahan v. Gulferews, 255 So. 2d 63, concerning a 48-year-old decedent earning $9,000 per year with a 17-year life expectancy, the court subtracted one-third for personal consumption, used a discount rate of 4–6 percent, and awarded:

Widow	$107,625
Daughter	45,500
	$153,125

Here, _____'s earnings would be higher, and his life expectancy is three times longer.

On review of the cases, I would expect a jury to return a verdict approximately in line with the expert's figures, and remittitur would appear to be unlikely.

Looking at the case through your eyes, plaintiff can easily establish a loss of yearly income of $10,000 for 45.5 years. Under cases, the jury would be entitled to increase this amount by at least a 3 percent inflationary rate. (See *Sylvester v. Liberty Mutual Ins. Co.*, 237 So. 2d 431, 3d (1970), holding that the decreasing purchasing power of the dollar may be considered in making award. See also Judge Rubin's approach in *In re Sincere Navigation Corp.*, 329 FS 652, O.C. La. (1971.) Applying a discount rate of 5 percent would make a new discount of 2 percent. Ten thousand dollars a year for 45.5 years discounted at 2 percent in $296,896. At a discount rate of 4 percent and a net discount of 1 percent the award is $328,040. This is using very conservative figures.

After you and your clients have reviewed these materials and reached your evaluation of this case, I would like to discuss settlement again.

Very truly yours,

8-4 SETTLEMENT BROCHURE

_____, widow of _____, et al.

v.

_____ Motor Line, et al.

I. Liability
    Exhibit   1. State police report
    "   2. Witnesses statements
    "   3. Report of arrest
    "   4. Newspaper reports

II. Facts of Death and Heirship
    Exhibit   5. Dixon Hospital emergency room report
    "   6. Coroner's report
    "   7. Death certificate
    "   8. Marriage certificate
    "   9. Birth certificate   —Abraham J. _____
    "   10. "_____"   —Joseph J._____
    "   11. "_____"   —Betty _____

III. Damages—Background Information
    Exhibit 12. Pictures—A.J. _____and family
    "   13. Statement—Betty _____—widow
    "   14. Character statement—Mike and Doris
    "   15. Character statement—Mrs. Louis
    "   16. Letter of commendation—U.S. Army
    "   17. Sympathy letters
    "   18. Physical examination of Joseph
    "   19. Physical examination of Betty
    "   20. Application for employment and employment achievement records.

IV. Damages—Monetary Figures
    Exhibit 21. Summary of amount of damages—Betty _____and Joseph
    "   22. Mortality table
    "   23. Calculations of loss of earning capacity and earning benefits—Table 1
    "   24. Decedent's income tax returns—1967-70
    "   25. T.G.&Y. employment information and estimated earnings, letter dated April 3, 1972

Forms in Chapter 9

9 | Trial Preparation

I. General

Trial preparation begins immediately, when the lawyer identifies the problems of the case, how they can be solved, and the best way to maximize the case's settlement potential and/or increase the chances of winning the trial. The settlement brochures and other settlement techniques provide the basic material for the final preparation, but all trial preparation makes use of the previous work done at earlier stages.

The legal theories normally should be mastered first so that proper factual preparation can be done. Identify all issues in the case and simplify them, reducing them to their essentials. Prepare a checklist of the various elements of the case and possible defenses. Many times the complaint and answer can provide an excellent checklist. Research the law applicable to each element identified. Once the legal requirements are determined, the investigation and preparation can proceed.

II. Game Plan

Goals and Objectives

Take time to think about the case and what you are trying to accomplish. How do you best go about presenting the case? What factors or techniques will be most successful in persuading the trier of fact, be it judge or jury?

It is important to have a comprehensive theory of the case, as well as alternative approaches, so that contingencies can be met at any stage of the trial. It is nearly impossible to persuade someone to adopt your point of view when (1) your own position is not clearly defined or (2) you don't actually have one.

Strategic Implications

1. <u>Adverse facts.</u> Normally it is best to purposely bring out adverse facts so that any damage can be minimized. Likewise, a confession and avoidance can sometimes turn damaging facts into a positive asset. The best rule is to admit those facts that will eventually be proven so that you, the lawyer, can control the impact of adverse material. In addition, you must take care to prepare the best possible responses so that you can meet other adverse facts that may surface.

2. <u>Routine facts and evidence.</u> Considerable time can be saved in both preparation and trial by admitting or stipulating to certain undisputed facts and/or agreeing to allow each side to present certain types of evidence—for example, copies of documents rather than originals.

3. <u>Exhibit.</u> It is often useful in cases involving multiple documents to premark each exhibit. At the same time the practitioner should develop a strategy involving one or more alternatives for authenticating documentary evidence and introducing each into evidence at the time of trial. Where documentary evidence must be authenticated by and introduced through witnesses, the mechanics of authenticating and introducing documentary evidence should be reviewed in advance with the witness.

4. <u>Objections.</u> An objection strategy must be developed as part of the case plan. Analyze the opposing side's case and the tendencies of the opposing lawyers and the judge. Then develop strategies to meet objectionable evidence and tactics in positive ways, which not only keeps out the improper evidence but does so in a way that advances the case as well. Motions in limine and other evidentiary motions should be considered so that objections are presented at the earliest possible time and before inappropriate evidence is brought to a jury's attention.

5. <u>What if.</u> The what-if game as part of trial preparation involves considering what to do if certain things happen. Many problems that do occur at trial can be easily solved by your being aware of them ahead of time and devising possible solutions. Preplanning of this nature will also uncover unrecognized weaknesses in the case and enable you to take steps to avoid problems before trial.

6. <u>Credibility problems.</u> These come in three forms—the parties, the lawyers, and the witnesses. Identify any credibility problems and determine the effect on your theory of the case, whether harmful or beneficial. Examine alternative ways to deal with the present problem and determine the most effective solutions.

Know Your Judge and Trier of Fact

Any good trial plan must take into account the likes, dislikes, and prejudices of the persons who will actually make the decisions in the case. Decide the best approach to persuade them—factual, legal, equitable, rational, reasonable, emotional, or sympathetic—or combinations of these. Likewise, identify those approaches that will not work or that may actually hurt your presentation. Consider the social context in which the case is being tried, the composite tendencies of the jurors, and how these factors could affect the outcome. A good case, even though it is well presented, will fall on deaf ears if (1) it runs contrary to what appeals to the judge, or (2) it is presented in a manner that is against the prevailing views of the community. Many jurisdictions now have books containing interviews with or information regarding the judges.

Know Your Adversary

It is also important to know your opposing counsel. What are his or her strengths, weaknesses, prejudices, and tendencies? In what manner does he or she prepare and try a case? Does he or she tend to settle cases or try them, and does this tendency make a difference? How does he or she relate to the judge and jury? Is there anything about the opponent and his or her approach that can be used to your advantage? Is there anything about the opponent's approach that can cause special problems that need attention?

III. Theory of the Case

"What is this case all about?" "Why should anyone care?" Not the fifteen-page legal brief answer or the twenty minute opening statement answer: but the clear, simple one or two sentence answer. *That* is your "theory of the case." If you cannot easily express it that way, you need to reexamine the case until you can.

The theory or theme of your case is the central, unifying principle upon which you should receive a judgment. Everything that you present at trial should relate to this theme. To be persuasive, it is important to be consistent. Develop a theory of the case that the judge and jury can identify and follow as the case unfolds.

Legal Theory of Recovery or Defense

The legal theory or theories are the framework for the presentation of the evidence. What you present and how you present it must always be in the context of the legal theory of the case. Use of the complaint or a checklist of the legal evidentiary requirements to support each theory of recovery or defense will help you avoid overlooking important details in both preparation and presentation of the case. As each requirement is prepared or met during trial, it can be checked off to make sure nothing is overlooked.

Factual Theory

The facts should be simplified and narrowed down to only those facts that relate to the theme or that prove that your version of what happened is more true than not. Consequently, it is important to develop factual theories that are consistent and that persuade the jury that your presentation of the facts is correct. Outline your burden of proof setting forth the supporting facts, the manner of proof, and any key questions and problems for each legal issue. Where alternate theories are used, develop alternative plans.

Fall-back Theory

Whenever possible, develop alternate plans and theories as part of the trial game plan so that the case is not lost when it becomes necessary to make adjustments during the trial.

IV. Witness Preparation

Favorable Witnesses

1. <u>Take the time.</u> Being a witness is a strange and unnatural experience for most people. Not surprisingly, therefore, many cases are won or lost on witness preparation. Take the time to do it right (see, for example, *Preparing Witnesses*, Daniel I. Small, ABA, 1998).
2. <u>Witness preparation memo.</u> Because many people are fearful of testifying in court, it is helpful to give them a memo to study that explains the procedure and some of the do's and don'ts of being a witness.
3. <u>Review key statements and depositions with key witnesses.</u> It is important to go over the statements and depositions of key witnesses with them. In this way, not only do the witnesses refresh their recollections, but the lawyer also has an opportunity to expand the discussion to cover other points that may have been overlooked or need

expansion At the same time, problem areas can be discussed so that the witnesses know what to expect and how to handle attacks on cross-examination.

4. Document Review. It is important to review each document or exhibit that will be introduced through the witness in order to familiarize the witness with the exhibit, *and* with the process of introducing documentary evidence to avoid pitfalls at trial.

5. Visit the scene with witnesses. This places the occurrence in its real context. Events leading up to the occurrence can also be explored in the actual context. Key distances can be measured or stepped off, and landmarks can be located in relation to each other. The witnesses can even reenact critical phases to determine the appropriate times and sequence of events. Many witnesses have problems on cross-examination because they have no idea of where things were at the scene or of how the facts are affected by the conditions at the scene.

6. Cross-examination. Cross-examine your own witnesses. In some cases, it is wise to take the witnesses to the courtroom and ask them questions so that they become familiar with the surroundings and can see for themselves that they are well prepared. Prepare the witnesses to handle certain types of cross-examination techniques they may encounter from the other side.

7. Mock examinations. A mock examination during which the witness is examined and cross examined as he or she would be at trial helps to highlight (and therefore address) weaknesses and to put the witness at ease. Using a tape recorder is helpful in showing the witnesses how they are wording an answer, how it can be used against them, and how the answer can be better stated. Such examinations are also helpful in teaching the witnesses how to pay attention to the question and then formulate an appropriate answer.

Adverse Witnesses-Cross-Examination Preparation.

1. Analysis. Determine the goals and objectives to be accomplished in each cross-examination. Preparation should include a review of the witness's statements and depositions and a comparison of his or her version of what occurred with your witness's versions and the results of your investigation. These should also be compared with the factual and legal theories to determine approaches that might work and what can be accomplished by cross-examination of the witness.

2. <u>Investigation.</u> Do you know everything you can about the other side's witnesses, both lay and expert? Carefully review their resume or other background information (including review with your client and/or expert) to see if anything seems unusual or exaggerated. Conduct a thorough search for other cases they have been involved in, either as a party or a witness, and review the case files or transcripts. Consider what other helpful information might be available.

3. <u>Checklist.</u> Finally, in preparing for cross-examination, a checklist of the points to be covered and the desired goals should be prepared. One method is first to modify the witness form to list the adverse points you expect the witness to make; then, next to it, list the possible countermeasures to be used to offset the effect of the points made by the witness. Any new points or admissions can also be included on the form, along with a list of appropriate exhibits to be covered.

V. Proof Charts

One effective way to focus your thinking and to match theory with reality is to use proof charts keyed to the basic elements of the case as guides to preparing and conducting a trial. Following are some examples. Sample forms are included to illustrate the techniques.

1. <u>Complaint, Answer, and Other Matters Summary Chart.</u> (See Form 9–1.) A summary or list of the elements that the plaintiff is required to prove is placed in numerical order on one side of a T-chart. The corresponding admissions, denials, and other items raised by the defense are listed on the other side of the T. This chart then provides, for ready reference, a quick summary of all points that are in dispute, as well as a list of admissions. In smaller cases the complaint itself, marked with "admit" or "deny" may serve the same function.

2. <u>Separate Element Pro and Con Chart.</u> (See Form 9–2.) Separate T-charts for each element of the case and each defense may be prepared covering the pros and cons of the evidence concerning each point necessary to establish the element. The list of points should be as complete as possible and should include a listing of the witnesses and exhibits to be used to establish or controvert the point.

3. <u>Individual Witness Pro and Con Chart.</u> (See Form 9–3.). A T-chart should be made up for each witness. Using the Complaint, Answer, and Other Matters Summary Chart as a guide, this chart is prepared by going through the case points in order and listing every point—both

favorable and unfavorable—to which the witness can testify and listing every exhibit that the witness can identify. It is imperative that this chart be complete so that nothing—good or bad—is overlooked.

This chart and the Separate Element Pro and Con Chart are really complementary because they each look at the case from a different perspective. As a result, the Separate Element Charts should be used in preparing the Individual Witness Pro and Con Chart to ensure that nothing is overlooked.

Once this chart has been completed for each witness, a decision can be made about whether to call the witness and what approach to use. With an adverse witness, the completed chart should indicate possible problems and highlight witnesses who are potential cross-examination risks.

4. Witness Examination Checklist. (See Forms 9–4 and 9–5.) In order to make certain that every point is covered, it is best to develop a witness chart or checklist for each individual witness, covering each point to be established or controverted and each exhibit to be used. Some lawyers do this by writing out the questions, and others do it by having a summary or outline of the points and a list of exhibits. There is no one-and-only way to do this; each lawyer should develop his or her own techniques.

This chart is actually a refinement of the Individual Witness Pro and Con Chart because it covers only those points that the lawyer actually intends to cover in the examination. Exhibits can then be premarked to conform to the checklist.

5. Order of Proof. Plan the presentation of the evidence to get the maximum persuasive effect. When dealing with opposing parties' witnesses or evidence, the order of attack should likewise be structured to provide the best possible effect. The plan for the order of proof should at least be written down in outline form for reference. (See Trial Outline Form 9–6.)

6. Master Exhibit List. (See Form 9–7.) This is a list, in numerical order of the documents and other exhibits to be used at trial. In complicated cases, the names of witnesses who will prove each exhibit may also be indicated. Files or notebooks may then be used to hold the documents in order, with the master exhibit list being used as an index. If there are a number of documents, an alphabetical cross-reference list may also be needed to help find documents quickly.

A place should be included to show whether the exhibit was admitted or denied so that before closing the case, it can be determined that all necessary exhibits have been admitted into evidence. The items that the judge will be asked to take judicial notice of, and whether notice is taken, can also be included on this list.

7. <u>Premarking Exhibits.</u> This permits preparation to proceed in an orderly fashion with the witnesses. The exhibit numbers can be entered in the witness checklist for each witness so that the proper exhibit can be available for use with that witness. This will save considerable time and has the advantage of showing, especially to a jury, that one is on top of one's case.

8. <u>Miscellaneous List.</u> (See Form 9–8.) Some items never really seem to fit in any specific list, but they still need to be noted in an appropriate place so that they are not overlooked. That is why it is frequently necessary to have a miscellaneous "to-do" list. Items such as admissions, judicial-notice points, stipulations, and other bits of information can be included on this list.

9. <u>Trial Notebooks.</u> A standard system of organizing documents, depositions and deposition summaries, research, pleadings, and exhibits is critical. As mentioned elsewhere here, one of the most successful techniques is to use notebooks. Ring binders allow for expansion as material is added, safe keeping of material entered, and ready removal of items for use. The number of notebooks and the way they are organized and indexed will depend on the size and complexity of the case.

VI. Conclusion: Trial Preparation Checklist

So much to do, so little time, so easy to forget! Everyone uses different mechanisms as reminders. To remind you of everything that must be done for trial, so key pieces don't slip through the cracks, you may wish to use a checklist, which you—and anyone else working on the case—should review regularly. A sample is enclosed as Form 9–9.

Further Reading

Bodin. *Civil Litigation and Trial Technique.* Ch. 5, "Final Preparation for Trial." New York: Practicing Law Institute, 1976.

Busch. *Law and Tactics in Jury Trials.* Ch. 11, "Preparation of the Case." Indianapolis, Ind.: Bobbs-Merrill, 1959.

Givens. *Advocacy*. Ch. 5, "Representing and Preparing a Witness"; Ch. 7, "Selection of Arguments"; Ch. 10, "Trial Strategies." Colorado Springs, Colo.: Shepard's/McGraw Hill, 1980.

Goldstein and Lane. *Goldstein Trial Technique*. Ch. 1, "Preparation for Trial: The Facts"; Ch. 2, "Preparation for Trial: The Personal Injury Case"; Ch. 3, "Preparation for Trial: The Contract Case"; Ch. 5, "Preparation for Trial: The Law and Pleadings." Mundelein, Ill.: Callaghan, 1969.

Hickam and Scanlon. *Preparation for Trial*. ALI-ABA, 1963.

Jeans. *Trial Advocacy*. Ch. 6, "Trial Preparation." St. Paul, Minn.: West Publishing Co., 1975.

Keeton. *Trial Tactics and Methods*. 2d ed., Ch. 2, "Direct Examination"; Ch. 9, "Preparation for Trial." Boston: Little, Brown and Company, 1973.

Kestler, *Questioning Techniques and Tactics*. Ch. 3, "Psychological Aspects of Questioning Strategy"; Ch. 9, "Total Witness Preparation." Colorado Springs, Colo.: Shepard's/McGraw Hill, 1982.

McCullough and Underwood. *Civil Trial Manual 2*. 2d ed., Ch. 10, "The Pretrial Conference." ALI-ABA, 1981.

Packel and Spina. *Trial Advocacy: A Systematic Approach*. Ch. 1, "Preparing for Trial"; Ch. 3, "Witness Preparation." ALI-ABA, 1984.

Small, Daniel. *Preparing Witnesses, A Practical Guide*. Chicago: ABA, 1998

Tanford. *The Trial Process*. Ch. 11, "Trial Preparation." Charlottesville, Va.:The Michie Co., 1983.

9-1 COMPLAINT, ANSWER, AND OTHER MATTERS SUMMARY CHART

1. Attach all pleadings and orders.
2. Underline all facts admitted, and outline.
3. Summarize or outline all disputed issues of law and fact.
4. Amend pleading or prayer, if necessary.

Complaint	Answer

Other Matters

9-2 SEPARATE ELEMENT PRO AND CON CHART

Element:

Pro	Witness/ Ex #	Con	Witness/ Ex #

9-3 INDIVIDUAL WITNESS PRO AND CON CHART

Witness Name: _____

Pro	Ex. #	Con	Ex. #

Witness Evaluation:

9-4 INDIVIDUAL WITNESS DIRECT EXAMINATION CHECKLIST

Points to Cover	Ex. # & Description

Possible Problems	Solutions

9-5 INDIVIDUAL WITNESS CROSS-EXAMINATION CHECKLIST

Adverse Points	Ex. #	Countermeasures	Ex. #

Other Points:

9-6 TRIAL OUTLINE

Enter preparation notes on left.   Enter trial notes on right.

Stage of Trail   **Time Est.**   **Trial Notes**

Preliminary motions: ___to___

Selection of jury: ___to___

Opening statement: ___to___

Plaintiff's witnesses/exhibits:

1. _____   ___to___
2. _____   ___to___
3. _____   ___to___
4. _____   ___to___
5. _____   ___to___
6. _____   ___to___
7. _____   ___to___
8. . _____   ___to___

Stage of Trail	Time Est.	Trial Notes

Defendant's witnesses/exhibits

1. _____   ___to___
2. _____   ___to___
3. _____   ___to___
4. _____   ___to___
5. _____   ___to___
6. _____   ___to___
7. _____   ___to___
8. . _____   ___to___

Rebuttal witnesses/exhibits

1. _____   ___to___
2. _____   ___to___
3. _____   ___to___

Final argument   ___to___

Instructions and motions   ___to___

9-7 MASTER LIST OF EXHIBITS

Exhibit #	Description	Witness	Status

9-8   MISCELLANEOUS ITEMS CHECKLIST

Admissions:

Judicial notice:

Stipulation:

Miscellaneous points:

Notes and reminders:

9-9 TRIAL PREPARATION CHECKLIST

A. Initial considerations.

   1. Complete preliminary review of entire file.

   2. Review prima facie case and defense requirements.

   3. Review individual case plan and goals.

   4. Research.
      a. Review issues and determine if further research is needed.
         1) Liability.
         2) Damages.
         3) Evidence.
         4) Other issues or potential problems.
      b. Update prior research.
      c. Prepare appropriate trial briefs and memos.

   5. Determine if additional investigation is needed.
      a. Facts.
      b. Damages.

   6. Discovery.
      a. Determine if any additional discovery is needed.
      b. Prepare and serve supplemental discovery forms to obtain updated information, especially witness names and addresses.
      c. Request updated expert-witnesses information and list of experts.

B. Settlement.

   1. Review prior settlement materials and efforts.

   2. Reevaluate settlement values and goals.

   3. Determine possibility of settlement.

   4. Plan settlement negotiation tactics.
      a. Determine when and how to approach other side.
      b. Plan case preparation considering settlement factors.
      c. Plan tactics to enhance the settlement possibilities.
      d. Attempt settlement negotiations before incurring major expenses.
      e. Plan settlement attempts around major preparation projects.
      f. Consider judge's position regarding settlement.

C. Game plan.

1. Trial goals and objectives.
    a. Determine the results to be accomplished.
    b. Determine how to best present the case.

2. Develop a comprehensive trial theory and alternatives.
    a. State problem in legal terms, such as, legal issues and propositions (legal theory).
    b. State goals, for example, client objectives.
    c. State tentative plan for achieving goals in terms of theory of case.
    d. Research legal issues and theory of case.
        1) Determine legal conditions or factual requirements (factual theory).
        2) Compare with list of known facts.
        3) Determine and list additional information or facts required.
    e. If legal conditions are satisfied without need for further information or facts, proceed to step *i* (below).
    f. If legal conditions are not satisfied and additional facts are required:
        1) Conduct further investigation for additional facts required.
        2) Redo statement of facts.
        3) Redo steps *a–e* (above).
        4) If required information or facts not obtained and legal conditions remain unsatisfied, proceed to step *g* (below).
    g. List and examine alternatives (fall-back theory).
        1) Who, what, why, when, and how.
        2) Reexamine alternatives in light of steps *a–f* (above).
    h. Restate the problem.
        1) Continuity, sequence, cause and effect.
        2) Similarity.
        3) Contrast.
    i. Finalize plan for achieving goals in terms of theory of case.
    j. Develop strategy for implementing plan; organize steps in presentation of proof.

3. Strategic implications.
    a. Admissions.
        1) Determine how to deal with adverse facts.
        2) Determine if routine facts can be admitted or stipulated.
    b. Objections.
        1) Determine theory and plan for possible objections.
        2) Prepare appropriate briefs and motions.

    c. Plan what, when, and how to attack opponent's case.

    d. Consider each side's credibility problems.

       1) The parties.

       2) The witnesses.

       3) The lawyers.

4. Study your judge and jury.

5. Study your adversary.

6. "What if"—Preplan approach to possible problems and potential surprises.

D. Witness preparation.

1. Favorable witnesses.

    a. Direct examination.

       1) Review witness explanation form with witness.

       2) Review the witness's statements and depositions with him or her as well as those of other key witnesses.

       3) Visit the scene with the witness.

    b. Cross-examination.

       1) Review potential problem areas with the witness.

       2) Consider tape-recorded mock examination to prepare witness.

       3) Visit courtroom with witness if necessary.

2. Adverse witnesses—cross-examination preparation.

    a. Determine goals of cross-examination of the witnesses.

    b. Review and compare witnesses' statements and depositions with those on other witnesses.

    c. Determine approaches that are most likely to be successful.

    d. Plan points to cover and appropriate questions.

E. Proof charts.

1. Complaint, Answer, and Other Matters Summary Chart.

2. Separate Element Pro and Con Chart.

3. Individual Witness Pro and Con Chart.

4. Witness Examination Checklist.

5. Order of Proof Chart.

6. Master Exhibit List.

F. Preparation schedules.

1. Office procedures regarding time requirements.
    a. Develop preparation plan with estimated time requirements.
    b. Chart out a time line for coordinated preparation management.
    c. Schedule work and assign tasks to staff.
    d. Review progress at predetermined times and make appropriate adjustments.
    e. Enter appropriate deadline dates on calendar.

2. Think time. As preparation progresses, set aside uninterrupted times to think about your case and how to present it.

G. Checklist of items to do or consider.

1. Are there any amendments to pleadings necessary or desirable?

2. Pretrial motions.
    a. Motions for summary judgment on all or some issues.
    b. Motions to obtain rulings on admissibility of evidence—offer of proof.
    c. Motions in limine—to exclude evidence or witnesses.
    d. Motions to compel attendance of witness or party.
    e. Motions to compel production of documents or evidence at trial.
    f. Motions to separate and/or exclude witnesses.
    g. Motions to limit experts to witnesses.
    h. Motions or demands to admit.
    i. Motions for the court to take judicial notice of certain evidence or facts.
    j. Motions for directed verdicts.
    k. Other items that are appropriate for judicial determination.

3. Pretrial conferences—use to advance preparation.
    a. Pleadings—amendments, summary judgments, and so forth.
    b. Facts—agreements regarding presentation of facts and/or stipulations regarding facts.
    c. Exhibits—agreements regarding admission and handling of exhibits, documents, and so on.
    d. Witnesses.
        1) Have subpoenas issued and served along with necessary fees.
        2) Schedule witnesses for preparation and trial appearances.
        3) Experts.
    a) Prepare and schedule.

    b) Make necessary travel arrangements.

        4) Consider evidence depositions for witnesses with availability problems.

    e. Depositions, statements, and the like.

        1) Abstract or summarize as appropriate.

        2) Obtain rulings regarding evidence and deposition objections prior to trial.

        3) Index key points.

4. Evidence.

    a. Assemble and review all evidence to be used or considered for use.

    b. Prepare all models, charts to be used as demonstrative evidence.

    c. Determine and prepare foundation requirements as necessary.

    d. Premark all exhibits and list on master list.

    e. Organize exhibits and documentary evidence for presentation.

    f. Make sure viewers, projectors, blackboards, easel are available in the courtroom.

    g. Obtain preliminary rulings on offers of proof before trial.

    h Consider quantity and quality of evidence. Is it plausible and reasonable? Is it cumulative?

    i. Determine how to deal with problems due to conflicts and inconsistencies.

    j. Is corroboration available and persuasive?

    k. Should any evidence be saved for rebuttal?

    l. Obtain authority to support or meet expected objections.

    m. Determine problem areas and how to avoid or minimize them.

    n. Consider limitations on numbers of witnesses and agreements regarding qualifications, and other factors.

    o. Can any legal issues be resolved or simplified; should any issues be briefed?

    p. Can any agreements be made regarding damage and evidence thereof? Are appropriate bills and documents available?

    q. Determine if any special problems exist and how they will be handled.

    r. What else is needed to coordinate or facilitate presentation of evidence in the trial?

5. Arguments.

    a. Outline opening statement as preparation progresses; use catch words.

    b. Draft final argument as theories are developed; test against evidence.

    c. Draft or outline probable opposing arguments; prepare evidence or arguments to offset.

    d. Have alternative arguments ready to cover potential problems.

6. Jury instructions.
    a. Prepare pattern instructions and use in preparing case and arguments.
    b. Determine if special instructions are needed; draft and obtain legal authority to support use.

Forms in Chapter 10

10 | Voir Dire and Jury Selection

Voir dire (literally, "to speak the truth") is the means by which counsel for the parties are provided information concerning prospective jurors. One purpose of voir dire is to obtain the information to support challenges to individual jurors. The information elicited may provide the grounds to challenge one or more persons for cause. In most cases, the information will be used in determining which persons should be subject to peremptory challenges.

I. Considering Voir Dire

There are four types of challenges to the jury:

1. Challenge to array, for example, to the entire jury panel, for defects in selection or summoning.
2. Challenge for cause (statutory)—age, citizenship, relationships.
3. Challenge to the favor (often also called "for cause") discretionary with court. Probable bias, prejudice, hostility because of background or relationship.
4. Peremptory challenge.

In most federal courts, voir dire questions are posed by the judge, based in part on requested questions submitted by counsel. These requests are an important part of your trial preparation and strategy. In many other courts, all or part of the voir dire questioning is conducted by counsel for the parties. This is an extraordinary chance to develop a rapport with the jury in a way not available once the jury has been empaneled. At no other time during the trial will counsel enjoy the opportunity to essentially engage in conversation with members of the jury.

Voir dire enables counsel, within limits, to educate the jury concerning the nature of the case, the parties' respective positions, and any special problems of the case that can be minimized by early exposure and explanation. Care must be taken not to exceed the bounds of propriety by commenting on the evidence or making argument.

Finally, voir dire provides information that may be quite valuable in determining how to persuade the jury of the merits of your client's position. Since the techniques that are useful for persuasion will vary depending on the composition of the group to be persuaded, you will want to use all that you have learned during voir dire once the jury is empaneled.

Many courts now have jurors fill out a jury questionnaire, which can give you invaluable information as a starting point for voir dire. Make sure to work with the clerk to get any questionnaires as soon as possible.

The first step in developing an effective voir dire is to decide what characteristics the most favorable and least favorable juror would have. The characteristics you choose to consider and the weight you attribute to each will depend on:

- the facts of your particular case;
- the issues and your theory of the case;
- the client you represent;
- the faith you have in the predictive value of various factors.

After determining the above, try to describe your most favorable juror and least favorable juror in terms of some or all of the following characteristics:

- marital status;
- parental status;
- residence ownership and neighborhood;
- family educational history;
- family occupational history;
- income level;
- family injuries, sickness, or disability;
- political leanings or affiliations;
- union and lodge affiliations;
- prior litigation and result;
- prior jury service and result;
- other status related to case facts.

Whether you use these factors or others, you will need to decide what you are looking for and what you do not want in a juror in order to develop questions that will be helpful in evaluating prospective jurors.

Before you actually prepare your questions, consider how the voir dire will be conducted and how you will exercise your challenges. For example:

A. Consult whatever statutes or local rules govern the conduct of voir dire, and check on any local customs that may control.
   1. Will the court conduct the voir dire with no opportunity for counsel to question prospective jurors?
   2. Will the court permit counsel to conduct the voir dire or at least permit follow-up questions?
   3. If the court will allow counsel to conduct some or all of the voir dire, how much time will the court permit?
B. How many peremptory challenges will you have?
C. Will challenges alternate between plaintiff and defendant?
D. How will empty spots be filled?
   1. By jurors in box moving up?
   2. By new juror from pool coming in?
   3. After each challenge?
   4. After each round of challenges?
E. If you accept panel without challenge at any time, can you challenge any of those jurors in a later round?

Once you have decided what characteristics you would like to have and which you would like to avoid in jurors and have determined the procedure that will be followed during voir dire, you are ready to prepare the actual questions. Your primary goal in preparing the voir dire is to design questions that will elicit the information you need to challenge jurors you do not want and to keep jurors you do want. There are, however, other considerations.

You must keep in mind that the manner of questioning should enable you to develop a rapport with the jury. Some types of questions—though the answers might prove useful—do more to alienate prospective jurors than to enlighten counsel. For example, to inquire directly concerning someone's religious views may well alienate either the person being questioned or other prospective jurors who consider the question offensive. A question concerning the groups or organizations with which the person most closely identifies may well provide the information you seek without seeming offensive.

In addition, consider the degree to which you need to, and will be permitted to, indoctrinate or educate the prospective jurors. If you represent a plaintiff who has fully recovered from his or her injuries but who suffered considerable pain for a long time in the process, you may wish to construct a question that makes this fact known and asks whether anyone has moral or religious objections to compensating an injured victim in such circumstances.

Finally, consider which types of questions should be asked of the venire collectively and which should be addressed individually.

A. General considerations.
  1. List topics of inquiry.
    a. Information about jurors.
    b. Information about case and conditioning questions—big case, amount, liability issues.
  2. List specific questions if necessary.
    a. Use open-ended questions so juror will express self.
    b. Use conversational approach, as if this were an initial social meeting.
    c. Ask questions that relate to juror's daily experiences, such as, "What do you do on the job?"
B. Obtaining information about jurors—basic areas of inquiry.
  1. Financial interest.
    a. Any direct benefit or detriment from the result.
    b. Taxpayer of defendant municipality.
    c. Shareholder, director, or officer of party corporation or mutual company (or is spouse?).
  2. Relationship to parties or counsel.
    a. Within degree prescribed by statute.
    b. Partner, employee, or competitor.
    c. Debtor, creditor, or customer.
    d. Landlord or tenant.
    e. Member of same or conflicting organization.
    f. Friend or enemy.
  3. Fixed opinion for or against.
    a. Type of action or defense.
    b. Race, nationality, occupation, or gender of party or important witness.
    c. Corporations, banks, governmental bureaus, and agencies.
    d. "Circumstantial" evidence.
    e. Capital punishment.
    f. Guilt or innocence.
    g. Plaintiffs or defendants.
    h. Law enforcement officials.

4. Knowledge of the case.
   a. Sources (news media, personal knowledge, hearsay).
   b. Extent (in general terms).
   c. Influence of such knowledge.
   d. Served on jury at previous trial or on grand jury that indicted a party.
   e. Familiarity with location, situation, or other facts.
5. Which way will juror lean?
   a. If served as juror before, what kind of case and result?
   b. Previously involved in similar case or claim as party or witness (or was member of family?).
   c. Occupation of juror and spouse.
   d. Job or business connection, past or present, relating to subject or party, for example, insurance work.
   e. Education, training, or hobby making him or her either valuable or a "pseudo-expert."
   f. Any training or courses in law.
   g. Marital or family status and history bearing on the issues.
   h. Economic status indicating identification or antipathy.
   i. Member of groups or organizations that may influence outlook.
   j. Additional consideration in malpractice actions.
      1) Association with organizations that support medical care.
      2) Personal beliefs and experiences with medical care.
      3) Personal or family connections with doctors and hospitals.
6. Reasons why couldn't serve on extended case.
C. Informing jurors about case.
   1. Bring out any special problems in case.
      a. Concerning client or witness (examples).
         1) Nonresident of community.
         2) Client is only witness or won't testify.
         3) Intoxication or drugs.
         4) "Different" in appearance or demeanor.
         5) Criminal record (if admissible).
         6) Notorious in community.
         7) History of mental disorders.
         8) Client or adversary is a corporation, large institution, religious organization, prominent figure, or member of high esteem profession.

     9) Children or accomplices as witnesses.

    10) Race, nationality, or literacy.

    11) Number of previous or subsequent accidents or injuries.

  b. In outlining case (examples):

    1) Explain preponderance-of-evidence rule.

    2) Why "excessively" large damages asked. Plaintiff—obtain juror agreement that willing to "award damages equal to injuries and the financial loss, even though it would require a large verdict."

    3) Serious or sympathetic injuries or cause of action. Defendant—"Plaintiff must prove case by greater weight of evidence, so, if evidence is equal, would you give plaintiff benefit of doubt because of (sympathetic factors)?"

    4) Long trial anticipated or technical evidence.

    5) Depositions in lieu of witness.

    6) Special defenses, such as, contributory negligence.

    7) Short on demonstrative or expert evidence.

    8) You must call openly hostile witness.

    9) Numerous technical objections must be made.

    10) Detailed medical evidence of injuries must be presented.

    11) Guest suing host.

    12) Relative suing relative.

    13) Action on oral contract.

    14) Patient suing doctor.

    15) Confession or admission by threat, force, or deceit.

2. Anticipate opponent's questions.

  a. Keep jurors by reaffirming freedom from bias. Use negative leading questions—"Of course, you aren't prejudiced."

  b. Dissimilarities of juror's experience.

3. Conditioning questions—plaintiff approach.

  a. Used to educate jurors or talk out of prejudices rather than eliminate.

  b. Introduce jurors to *theme* of case.

  c. Big case—important issues.

  d. Juror's luck and honor to sit on case.

  e. Lose honor if participate in big case with defendant verdict.

  f. Identification with plaintiff as a class—such as, pedestrians.

4. Conditioning question—defendant approach.

  a. Condition jury to antiplaintiff theme—such as, malingering.

      b. Big case for defendant—unfairness of complaint.

      c. Identify defendant with group or industry—establishment argument.

   D. Use prepared ending to stop, which indicates to jury that desired ends accomplished.

No abstract discussion of voir dire can anticipate all questions that should be included for a specific trial. Examples of questions that might be included in an automobile personal injury case are set forth at Form 10–1.

II. Conducting Voir Dire

The manner in which you conduct voir dire must be governed by your own style. The primary thing to keep in mind is that you are trying to elicit information in a manner that will help you establish a rapport with the prospective jurors. While you probably will be somewhat casual and informal in your questioning, you will want to gain the prospective jurors' respect for your professional demeanor.

   A. General suggestions for conducting voir dire examination:

     1. Introductory points.

      a. Introduce yourself, parties, other lawyers, witnesses (developing rapport).

      b. Explain briefly what the case is about and what the issues are (informing jurors about case).

      c. Explain that it is your duty to ask questions of prospective jurors to ensure that both sides will get a fair trial (developing trust).

      d. Assure them that if any are excused, it is not a reflection on them. As we all know, it is quite natural that the associations or experiences we have had will sometimes cause any of us, quite unconsciously, to lean more toward one side than the other (developing trust).

     2. Develop interest through variety.

      a. Move from juror to juror with each question.

      b. Do not question jurors in order; move randomly.

      c. Vary form of question from juror to juror.

      d. Intersperse question to entire panel with individual questions.

Since it is difficult to effectively conduct voir dire while taking notes, have someone at counsel table record each prospective juror's answers, if that is possible. Take these notes on a standardized form that can be easily used later during the process of striking prospective jurors (See Form 10–2). An additional form set up like the jury box can be useful for recording your subjective reactions to each person, although such forms are rarely large enough to record all observations (See Form 10–3).

III. Exercising Challenges

When the time comes to exercise your peremptory strikes, it is extremely important to keep close track of your strikes as well as the strikes of your adversary. You also will need to consider the effect of each strike. For example, will striking one person merely result in the substitution of an even less desirable juror?

It is also important to seek the input of your client. While you may not choose to forgo striking a particular person on the advice of your client, you might strike someone who is offensive to your client, even if you find the person acceptable.

There are no fixed guidelines that can tell you which persons to strike and which to retain in any particular case. One rule that seems to have universal acceptance, however, is that you should strike any person for whom you feel dislike, for whatever reason. If you find someone offensive, there is a good chance that he or she feels the same way about you and would not be favorably disposed toward your case.

General suggestions for exercising challenges are:

A. Testing observation and intuition. Give questionable juror a simple command, such as, "Sit back and relax," and see reaction for hostility.
B. Measure potential jurors against ideal, and strike least desirable first.
C. Challenge any juror you personally dislike.
D. Foundation for challenges for cause.
   1. Develop any area of relationship or bias in depth.
   2. Use leading questions to establish influence, preconceived ideas, prejudice.
   3. Develop questions to allow juror a graceful way to remove himself or herself.
E. Accept panel and leave to defendant to challenge.
F. Do not exhaust all available challenges; reserve one.

Further Reading

ABA Section of Litigation. *The Litigation Manual: A Primer for Trial Lawyers* 152–56. Chicago: ABA, 1983.

Anderson. "Psychotherapy Techniques in Voir Dire Selection." *Trial* 52–55 (September 1980).

Fahringer. "Voir Dire: A View From the Defense." 189 *N.Y.L.J.* 2 (1983).

Gold. "Voir Dire: Questioning Prospective Jurors on Their Willingness to Follow the Law." 60 *Ind. L.J.* 163–90 (1985).

Jeans. *Trial Advocacy* 162–95. St. Paul, Minn.: West Publishing Co., 1975.

Jordan. *Jury Selection.* New York: McGraw-Hill, 1980.

Kelner, "Jury Selection: The Prejudice Syndrome." *Trial* 48–53 (July 1983).

Mauet. *Fundamentals of Trial Techniques* 23–47. Boston: Little, Brown and Company, 1980.

McGarry. "Do-it-Yourself Voir Dire." 10 *Litigation* 38 (1984).

Morrill. *Trial Diplomacy* 1–21. Court Practice Institute, 1978.

Paul. *Materials on Juries and Jury Research: An Annotated Bibliography.* American Judicature Society, 1977.

Ring. "Voir Dire: Some Thoughtful Notes on the Selection Process." *Trial* 72–75 (July 1983).

Ritter. "Practical Aspects of Voir Dire and Medical Malpractice." *Personal Injury Annual* 258–70 (1983).

Turley. "Voir Dire: Preparation and Execution." 8 *Litigation* 19–23 (1982).

Van Dyke. *Jury Selection Procedures: Our Uncertain Commitment to Representative Juries.* Ballinger, 1976.

Wagner. *Art of Advocacy: Jury Selection.* New York: Matthew Bender, 1981.

Werchick, Arne. "Method Not Madness: Selecting Today's Jury." *Trial* 65–70 (December 1982).

Wiseman. "Lawyer Voir Dire." 11 *Litigation* 5–6 (1984).

10-1 SAMPLE VOIR DIRE QUESTIONS: MVA CASE

The following are merely examples of questions you might wish to include in an automobile personal injury case:

1. Where do you live?
2. How long have you lived at that address?
3. Do you own your home or rent?
4. How old are you? (Probably best asked by court in order to avoid having attributed to you any embarrassment the question may cause.)
5. What is your marital status?
6. How long have you been married to Mr./Mrs. _____?
7. How did you meet Mr./Mrs. _____? (This may provide useful information concerning social habits.)
8. Do you have any children?
9. Are any of your children employed? or, Where do your children work?
10. Do any of your adult children live at home? (Adult children at home may influence parental views on various issues.)
11. Where did you grow up?
12. Where did your spouse grow up?
13. What did you parents do (for a living)?
14. Did circumstances permit you to attend college?
15. If so, what college(s) did you attend, and for how long? (Length of attendance and occupation will probably give you a good idea of whether the person graduated.)
16. Where do you work?
17. What does your work for the *XYZ* Company involve?
18. How long have you worked for that company?
19. What does your spouse do?
20. What does your spouse's work for the *XYZ* Company involve?
21. How long has your spouse worked for the *XYZ* Company?
22. What types of hobbies or recreational activities do you (and your spouse) like to engage in?
23. Do you (and your spouse) drive?
24. What kinds of vehicles do you have?
25. Do you recall what bumper stickers you have on the car you drive? (if they have any that they are embarrassed to reveal in court, they probably will say they do not recall. Otherwise, they will say none or tell you which ones they have. Some can be very revealing of affiliations and societal prejudices.)
26. Do you have one or more favorite magazines that you read on a regular basis? (This permits the juror who does not read to answer truthfully

that he or she has no favorites without admitting to not reading any magazines.)

27. Do you have one or more favorite books that you have read and, if so, which ones?

28. Do you have a favorite television program?

29. Do you have a favorite radio station?

30. Do you have one or more favorite movies?

31. If you had your choice of a game to play with someone, what would it be?

32. What do you enjoy doing on weekends and holidays?

33. Do you ever drink on social occasions with your friends? (This question may have little use in cases that do not involve the use of alcohol but could be helpful in other cases to identify some persons holding strong religious views.)

34. What qualities do you most admire in other people?

35. How do you feel about labor unions?

36. Have you or any member of your family ever been a member of a labor union? If so, who and which labor unions?

37. Have you or any member of your family ever been active in any political organization? If so, who and which organizations?

38. Are you active in any social or civil organizations? If so, which ones?

39. Have you or any member of your family ever been the victim of an automobile crash?

40. Do you know anyone who has ever been the victim of an automobile crash?

41. Have you or any member of your family ever been a party to a lawsuit?

42. Have you or any member of your family ever testified in a lawsuit?

43. How do you feel about persons who bring lawsuits to obtain relief when some other person or company has caused them injury?

44. If some other person or company injured you, would you have any reluctance to bring a lawsuit to be compensated for the harm done to you?

45. Have you ever served as a juror before? If so, in what types of cases, criminal or civil, have you served as a juror? Was a verdict reached by each of the juries on which you served?

46. When was the last time you served on a jury, and what type of case was it?

47. Have you ever served as the foreperson of a jury?

48. Have you or any member of your family ever studied law, either formally or informally?

49. Have you or any member of your family ever studied medicine, either formally or informally? (This same type of question should be asked as to any discipline that is involved in your case.)

50. Are any of your friends or close acquaintances lawyers or doctors?

51. I realize that people often consult lawyers for very personal reasons, and I don't wish to pry, so would you tell us without stating the reason whether you have ever consulted or used a lawyer for any reason other than to obtain a will? (You may wish to ask the same question regarding family members.)

52. Which lawyer did you consult? (This information frequently will give you an idea as to the nature of the person's legal problem.)

53. This is a lawsuit in which my client, John Doe, contends that the defendant, Mr. Jones, negligently ran a red light and crashed into John's car, seriously injuring John. Do any of you know, or are any of you acquainted with, John or Mr. Jones?

54. Do any of you know or have any of you read or heard anything about this collision?

55. Do any of you know or are any of you acquainted with Mr. Jones's lawyer, Mr. Slick, or any of the following lawyers in Mr. Slick's law firm?

56. Do any of you know or are any of you acquainted with His Honor Judge Dogood?

57. Are any of you or any members of your family stockholders of the *ABC* Insurance Company?

58. Are any of you or any members of your family related by blood or marriage to any of the officers or directors of the *ABC* Insurance Company?

59. Do any of you have close friends or acquaintances who are or have been employed by an insurance company?

60. Do any of you have any reason—which you need not state—for not wanting to serve as a juror in this case, which is expected to last _____ days?

10-2 JURY SELECTION

1. Attach jury list with notes
2. Juror profile—do not want:

	No.____	No.____	No.____	No.____	No.____
Name:_____	_____	_____	_____	_____	_____
<u>Challenges:</u>	_____	_____	_____	_____	_____
<u>Background:</u>	_____	_____	_____	_____	_____
Police	_____	_____	_____	_____	_____
Med	_____	_____	_____	_____	_____
Ins	_____	_____	_____	_____	_____
Teach	_____	_____	_____	_____	_____
Realty	_____	_____	_____	_____	_____
Army	_____	_____	_____	_____	_____
Bank	_____	_____	_____	_____	_____
	_____	_____	_____	_____	_____
<u>Experience:</u>					
Accident	_____	_____	_____	_____	_____
Injury	_____	_____	_____	_____	_____
Sue-Sued					
Witness	_____	_____	_____	_____	_____
Fam. Inj.	_____	_____	_____	_____	_____
Driver	_____	_____	_____	_____	_____
	_____	_____	_____	_____	_____
	_____	_____	_____	_____	_____
<u>Marital:</u>	_____	_____	_____	_____	_____
<u>Children:</u>	_____	_____	_____	_____	_____
Court Exp:					
Civ.	_____	_____	_____	_____	_____
Crim.	_____	_____	_____	_____	_____
Personality:					
Likeable	_____	_____	_____	_____	_____
Smiling	_____	_____	_____	_____	_____
Sour	_____	_____	_____	_____	_____
Dull	_____	_____	_____	_____	_____
Smart	_____	_____	_____	_____	_____

10-3 VOIR DIRE OUTLINE

Questions   Authority

Form in Chapter 11

11-1. Opening Statement Checklist

11 | Opening Statement

I. Purpose of Opening Statement

The opening statement will be your first opportunity to tell the jury what the case on trial is all about. The jury may have sat through hours of sometimes boring, repetitious questioning during jury selection. At last they are going to hear the story of the case. Their interest is at a peak. Your goal is to convince the jury to view your case and your client's from your perspective. Help the jury visualize your theories of the case. The opening statement is your first and best opportunity to persuade.

Accepted psychological and communication theories support the importance of first impressions. Trial lawyers agree that opening statements can and often do make the difference in the outcome of a case. The notion that jurors can completely suspend or reserve all judgment until the very end is unrealistic. Repeated studies and experience have demonstrated that the lawyer who "wins" the opening statement, in the great majority of cases, will ultimately receive a favorable verdict.

When preparing and delivering the opening statement, remember the four goals of every phase of trial:

- to transmit information that will educate the jury;
- to diffuse the harmful effects of the adverse features of the case;
- to develop rapport and enhance the credibility of both counsel and client; and
- to persuade the trier of fact.

Another very practical aspect of a well-prepared and effectively delivered opening is that it may favorably influence settlement negotiations after the start of trial.

Deliver a simple logical, dramatic, persuasive story that clearly presents the facts entitling your client to a favorable verdict. The statement should hold the jury's attention and motivate them to decide in your favor.

II. Preparation Issues

Timing

Whenever possible, you will want to know in advance how much time the court will allow you for opening statement. Some judges are very strict about adhering to time limits; others are not. There is no quicker way to lose trial momentum than to have the judge cut you off in the middle of your opening statement because you have exceeded the allotted time. You may be able to learn about your judge's preference at a pretrial hearing. If not, call the clerk, or ask other lawyers who have tried cases in front of your judge.

Particularly if your opening goes first (usually the plaintiff in a civil case, prosecution in a criminal case), you want to resist the court's normal desire to move cases more quickly by limiting the time for argument. Stand your ground and push for the time you need. At the same time, understand that opening statements will often be limited in time, and plan accordingly.

If you represent a defendant, you may have the opportunity to waive or reserve your opening until the close of the plaintiff's or prosecution's case. Lawyers sometimes come up with all kinds of strategic reasons to this. Don't buy it! Do not concede first impressions. Do not allow the other side to introduce its case and then put on its evidence without interruption and an alternative presentation of the facts and issues.

Notes

An age-old dispute: the "pros" and "cons" of using notes during opening statement. The pros seem obvious: they provide a clearer, more organized presentation; less chance that you will get lost or stumble; and a good crutch to overcome your nervousness. As attractive as these pros might sound, the cons are overwhelming. This is your first and best chance to talk *with* the jury. Do not forfeit it by talking *at* them. The problem with notes is the irresistible magnetic attraction that exists between your eyes and the written word. No matter how familiar you are with your case and your opening, if it is written down, you *will* read it. The result is not just lost eye contact, it is lost personal contact. We all read with a different voice than we talk. Juries know the difference, and they did not experience all the inconvenience of jury service just to have some strange lawyer read to them.

When you think about it, none of the pros for using notes are convincing. Juries are not looking for perfection, they are looking for commitment: do you believe in your case, and can you explain it to them and give them enough reasons to support you. Surely, by the time of trial, you know your case well enough to speak without reading. Talk directly to the jury, and nothing else matters.

- You're nervous? So what! You should be; trials are serious business. So are the jurors, and it will make them *less* nervous if they see that you are too. Deal with the symptoms of nervousness, and forget the disease itself: slow down, take a deep breath, hold on to something if you fidget, and then keep going.
- You might lose your place or stumble? So what! No one wants to talk to an automaton just because it does not make mistakes. Smile, apologize, and win the jury's hearts by being human.
- You might leave something out? Unlikely, but the answer is not to write out your opening. At most, if the case calls for it, do a one-page list of one or two key word points that you want to—or need to—make in you opening. Print it with lots of spacing and large-size type, leave it at counsel table and then try not to use it except as a quick reference if you get truly lost, or toward the end to make sure you have covered everything.

The irony here is clear. Lawyers who have had fewer trials will want to use notes more, and should in fact use them not at all, or much less. Lawyers with more experience who need notes less may be better able to benefit by them, particularly in complex cases.

Visual Aids

Too often, lawyers think about visual aids—whether its charts, diagrams, blowups of photos or documents, models, or whatever—as things to use with witnesses. However, as trial lawyers, particularly in opening statement, we are also teachers trying to teach a "class" of jurors a new subject and persuade them to accept our theories. You know from your own school experiences that we learn more effectively when we use more than one sense. The best teachers engage as many of our senses as possible to make their points. Why not do the same in the opening statement? Visual aids not only help you explain your case to the jury, but they bolster your personal credibility at this critical stage. Visual or concrete aids give support to your words and help the jury believe that when you say something, it is true.

Find ways to use visual aids in your opening, but work out the logistics in advance. First, get the court and opposing counsel's agreement (or the court's decision, if counsel won't agree), on what you can use. Then, walk through the physical logistics. Murphy's law applies to exhibits in the courtroom: "What Can Go Wrong, Will Go Wrong." Whatever you need—an easel, a pointer, a projector, a screen, or whatever —make sure that it is in the courtroom and you know how to set it up and work it, or bring your own.

Preparation Techniques

Everyone prepares differently for how to present during a trial, but there are some proven techniques that you should consider. Try explaining your case to nonlawyers. Don't just talk about your case with those who are working on it or other lawyer colleagues. Find uninvolved *non*lawyer friends, relatives, or even total strangers and try to explain your case to them convincingly. Doing this repeatedly, and listening both to what works and what questions you get, will help you to talk effectively to jurors.

III. Legal Issues

Elements

Make sure you know the key elements of what you have to prove (or rebut), and address each of them. Ignoring a key element can be embarrassing in the hands of a good opponent ("there's a good reason why plaintiff's lawyer didn't mention this key element in his opening . . ."), and in some jurisdictions it can put your case at risk. Make sure that you cover the essential ground.

Argument

One of the main differences between opening statement and closing argument is implied in the name: opening is supposed to be a straightforward statement of what the evidence will show, not argument. Opinions, inferences, and exhortations are supposed to be left for closing. That distinction is easily stated but not easily followed, and contains traps for the unwary.

First, know your local customs and your judge. I have given openings and closings in one part of the country that were considered relatively conservative and restrained by local standards, which would have been viewed as outrageously argumentative and improper in courtrooms elsewhere.

However, you do not have to travel across the country to see big differences in what is allowed: sometimes all you need to do is travel across the hall. Different judges have widely different views of what is allowable argument. You can put yourself—and your client—at real disadvantage by not finding out how far you can—and cannot—go.

Second, understand that "nonargumentative" does not mean boring. Some lawyers go too far to avoid argument and end up with a stiff, formal, emotionless presentation that will not convince anyone of anything. Be positive. Be vivid. Be dramatic. You can show your commitment to your case through your body language, your voice, your emotion, your phrasing, and other ways without venturing into improper argument. Just be grounded in fact, not opinion. If in doubt, make clear to all that you are just talking about what the evidence will show. However, don't feel that you have to say those magic words constantly.

Third, while arguing is a technical sin, exaggerating can be a mortal one. Understand the difference between being a strong advocate for your case and seriously overstating it. Juries don't really understand or care about what is or is not argumentative, but they certainly understand and care when someone lies to them about what the evidence will be. You can lose your credibility—and your case—by venturing too far into overstatement. If you hear an opponent exaggerating in opening statement, get a transcript from the court reporter. Then consider effective ways to use the exaggeration in closing argument or even in questioning witnesses.

IV. Content

Framework
There is an old adage about public speaking that goes "Tell them what you're going to say, say it, then tell them what you just said." This saying applies as well to an opening statement. You need to have a structure with a beginning, middle, and end that the jury can understand and follow easily. Moreover, you must give careful consideration to what goes into each part and how to communicate it most favorably and dramatically.

Beginning
Introduce yourself, your client, other key players as appropriate, and the case. For the personal introductions, decide up front who you are going to call what. Do you want to refer to your client by his or her first name, and if so will the court allow it? Is the other side Sam Smith, Mr. Smith,

Defendant Smith, or just "the defendant"? Make these decisions, then remain consistent.

To introduce the case, use the basic theme that you have developed, and will be referring to throughout. You may even introduce your theme with a "minitheme," a one or two word summary of the theme leading into the substantive theme. For example: "This is a case about greed. It's a case about. . . ."

Middle

One of the dangers trial lawyers face is that, having devoted time and energy to preparing the case, by the time of trial they know it too well. They are so familiar with the setting, the players, the background, and the facts that they speak in shorthand, thus leaving far behind anyone who has not been equally immersed in the case. Opening statement is your opportunity to begin the process of immersing the jury in the case, but to do so effectively you need to take a step back and make sure that you cover all the basics first. A helpful strategy for creating this overview for the jury is to follow the organization provided by your core documents discussed in Chapter 2. Whether done separately or in unison, you need to give the jury the following:

1. <u>Case Summary.</u> The jury needs to understand what the case is all about, why they should care about your client, what happened, and what the key issues are.
2. <u>Cast of Characters.</u> During the course of trial, the jury will hear lots of names. Opening statement is the time to make clear, from your perspective, who's who, and where they fit into the case. Whether you do this all at once or as people or entities come up in your statement, make sure that you do not leave anyone floating out there unidentified.
3. <u>Chronology.</u> At some point, you will probably want to take the jury through the facts chronologically. This is where visual aids may help the most, but do not substitute detail for drama: keep yourself and the jury focused on your central theme.

While you emphasize your positive theme, do not ignore your weaknesses. Every case has weaknesses, and if a jury is treated with respect and honesty, they will understand that. However, if you ignore your case's weaknesses they will not go away: they will only get worse. A minor, explainable problem can become a devastating blow if you allow the other side to argue that you tried to cover it up.

Be aware throughout your opening that it is the foundation of the case, and for the sake of clarity and credibility, you want that to be clear in every possible way. Design your opening so that the jury will hear echoes of it throughout the testimony. Then refer directly back to it at the time of closing argument. This kind of consistency can have a very positive impact on the jury.

Conclusion

Wrap up your opening statement by bringing the jury back to your key themes. Be dramatic and direct. Thank them for their time and attention, tell them what will happen next, then assure them that you will be back at the close of the evidence to ask them for the verdict you want based on the evidence. It is surprising how often lawyers fail to make this final connection. Tip O'Neal, the late Speaker of the U.S. House, used to speak of learning this lesson when he asked neighbors who he assumed would support him why they did not, and was told, "you never asked for our vote." Take Tip's political lesson to trial: never assume; always ask for their vote.

V. Legal Reminders

1. Check the law of your jurisdiction to see if the court can direct a verdict when the opening statement fails to set out a proper cause of action (read the pleadings to protect yourself).
2. A lawyer acting within the scope of his or her authority as the client's agent can make binding admissions during an opening statement that might be used by the adverse party. Once again, check your jurisdiction's case law.
3. An opening statement should not contain statements of fact that cannot be proven at trial. Avoid referring to "evidence" you know is inadmissible. This could create grounds for a mistrial, new trial, or reversal of a favorable verdict.
4. Generally, you are not permitted to discuss the law in any detail in an opening statement. Court permission may be secured, however, to discuss the general basis of some statutory causes of action (such as, strict liability acts, dram-shop, federal employers' liability).
5. Check applicable local law covering the wide variety of statements deemed improper (for example, direct appeal to sympathy, violation of collateral source rule, misstatement of evidence, addressing juror by name).

There is no universal opening statement. You should do what is best and most comfortable for you personally, your case, and your setting. However, considering what was just discussed in this chapter, there are some common points to consider. They are presented in Form 12–1, Opening Statement Checklist.

Further Reading
Colley, Michael F. "The Opening Statement: Structure, Issues, Techniques." *Trial Magazine.* November 1982.

Julien, Alfred S. *Opening Statements.* Wilmette, IL.: Callaghan, 1980–84.

Lane, Fred. *Goldstein Trial Technique.* 3d ed. Vol. 1, § 10.01. Wilmette, IL.: Callaghan, 1984.

Levin, Frederic G. *Effective Opening Statements.* Executive Reports Corporation, 1983.

Mauet, Thomas. *Fundamentals of Trial Techniques.* § 3.1. Boston: Little, Brown and Company, 1980.

Trine, William A. "Motivating Jurors Through Opening Statements." *Trial Magazine.* December 1982.

11-1 OPENING STATEMENT CHECKLIST

A. Purposes.

    1. To transmit information and educate.

    2. To diffuse harmful effects of adverse features.

    3. To develop rapport and enhance credibility.

    4. To persuade.

B. Preparation and delivery.

    1. Setting the stage.
       a. Introduction.
          1) Introduce parties—personalize client.
          2) Describe purposes of opening statement, where helpful.
             a) Analogize to jigsaw puzzle or road map.
             b) Remind jurors that opening statement is "not to be considered evidence," where appropriate.
          3) Describe stages of trial (if court has not done so).
          4) Explain burden of proof—preponderance of evidence rather than reasonable doubt.
          5) Explain role of counsel, jury, and judge.
          6) Explain importance of case to client—his or her day in court—to redress a wrong.
          7) Give <u>Theme</u>.
       b. History of parties and key witnesses.
          1) Give, for example, employment history; condition of health; activities at home, work, and recreation; or victim's history in relationship to defendant in criminal case.
          2) If suing in capacity of administrator, executor, trustee, or "next friend," explain to jury what this means.
       c. Scene of occurrence. Consider this in the broadest sense (for example, scene can encompass a wide variety of settings or scenarios, depending upon type of case being tried).
          1) Describe factors about the "scene" that help the case.
          2) Consider orienting the jury as to directions before beginning description of scene.
          3) Consider using demonstrative evidence to illustrate, if allowed.

    d. Instrumentality.

       1) Identify in broadest terms (for example, respirator in a malpractice case; the truck, train engine, or scaffold in any personal injury case).

       2) Describe feature of the "instrumentality" that supports your theory.

    e. Preexisting practices, procedures, or customs. Describe them if they help the case.

       1) Give jury an idea of customary behavior or standards for comparison of defendant's conduct.

       2) Refer to expert witnesses who will be called at trial, if appropriate.

    f. If defense counsel:

       1) Create interest in the differences between the two sides.

       2) Specifically, forcefully, and persuasively deny the charges made by plaintiff's counsel.

2. How it happened. Lay out the story of case fully, fairly, and in positive, forceful terms.

    a. Visualization.

       1) Describe what occurred in a logical and chronological order as seen by client.

       2) Use sufficiently descriptive words and gestures so jury "sees" transaction from your client's perspective.

       3) Defense counsel should describe same occurrence through his or her client's and key witnesses' eyes.

    b. Flashback technique.

       1) Use as excellent way of developing the picture of the incident.

       2) Lawyer utilizes by not mentioning or emphasizing certain facts to jury before describing what occurred.

       3) Use to highlight and develop background information that should have been described when setting the stage.

       4) Use to avoid charging client with certain knowledge that preexisted the occurrence; jury may believe a higher duty of care applies.

    c. Establish careless or wrongful conduct of defendant and blameless conduct of plaintiff.

       1) Was your client's conduct proper in every way?

       2) Was everything the defendant did reasonable under the circumstances?

       3) Can you persuade the jury the client had no choice?

       4) Could accident/dispute have been avoided y defendant? Your client? How?

3. Factual basis of liability/nonliability or guilt/innocence.
   a. Tell jury specific factual basis for your right to a verdict. Goal is to create persuasive impact using layman's language and nonverbal communication.
   b. Avoid conclusions such as "negligently operated his car," or "defendant violated his agreement." Use specific factual terms to enumerate the things the adverse party did wrong.
   c. Consider using key fact approach.
      1) Select key fact in dispute that you know you can prove.
      2) Stress importance of key fact in opening statement.
      3) Later prove and remind jury in closing argument.
      4) If you can disprove a single important fact of opposing party, do so with first witness following defendant's opening statement.
   d. Refer to statute if it is a basis of liability and if law of jurisdiction allows discussion in opening statement.
   e. Use demonstrative evidence, and refer to objects or people in courtroom if applicable and allowed by court.
   f. Emotional peak of opening statement—your voice and manner should reflect the strong feelings you have for your client's cause. Gestures, facial expressions, and use of the arms or body can be important.

4. Miscellaneous points to consider.
   a. Anticipate and refute defenses (plaintiff only).
   b. If appropriate, subtly impeach credibility of those witnesses, lay or expert, other party will rely upon during trial.
   c. Anticipate bad features and weaknesses of your case; preparing the jury by disclosing known weaknesses in your case will mitigate and diffuse harmful evidence and create credibility with jury, for instance:
      1) Client who will not testify—perhaps because prohibited by statute (dead man's statute).
      2) Missing witnesses and parties.
      3) Language problem—interpreters needed.
      4) Criminal or driving record.
      5) Intoxication or other impairment of physical or mental faculties—Stress other party's breach of duty or fault as direct cause regardless of client impairment.
   d. Humanize plaintiff's "affirmative defense conduct."
   e. Jury must *never* feel after opening statement that the lawyer has unfairly withheld information; carefully anticipate and refute if possible.

f. Caveat for criminal cases: Be very careful. Since defendant does not have the burden of proof, you are not required to present evidence, and this right may reach constitutional dimensions.

g. Remember plaintiff has no right of rebuttal in opening statements in civil cases.

5. Damages and injuries. Emphasize when liability is weak; be brief when liability is strong.

   a. Injuries. Do not exaggerate or misstate what you intend to prove.

     1) Explain the mechanics of the injury. Remember visualization.

     2) Describe anatomy of injured area.

     3) Define medical terms, contract terms, and so forth. (depends upon case), and phrases that may be used in testimony.

     4) Describe immediate signs and symptoms, first aid, and hospitalization.

     5) Describe diagnosis and treatment, including surgery and condition during treatment.

     6) Describe effect on employment and limitations on recreation, sports, everyday life, and activities (personalize plaintiff, similar to jurors). Create empathy.

     7) State prognosis for future.

   b. Damages.

     1) Declare that plaintiff is due just compensation.

     2) Itemize categories of damage.

       a) Medical.

       b) Hospital.

       c) Surgical.

       d) Transportation.

       e) Lost earnings and future earning capacity.

       f) Past, present, and future pain and suffering.

       g) Disfigurement.

       h) Inability to enjoy normal functions of life.

       i) Mental suffering.

       j) Humiliation, shame, embarrassment, or anxiety suffered.

       k) Loss of self-image as breadwinner.

     3) Explain normal life expectancy and compare to plaintiff's.

     4) If contract case, deal with damages aspects by continuing to plaintiff's activities relating to his or her damages, including his or her efforts to mitigate.

     5) If representing defendant, you should not discuss damage aspects of plaintiff's case except to deny responsibility for them. Avoid "We are sorry" statements if possible.

6) Conclude.
   a) Themes.
   b) Explanation of what comes next.
   c) Thank jury.
   d) Remind them: will ask for vote at end.

Forms in Chapter 12

12 | Direct Examination

Effective direct examination is one of the most overlooked and underrated litigation skills. Conducting good, clear direct examination can take an enormous amount of preparation, skill, and discipline. Yet direct has always taken second fiddle to its sexier, more adversarial flipside, cross-examination. Many lawyers, even experienced litigators, have never taken the time and effort to master direct examination technique. However, with work any lawyer can learn to conduct effective direct examination. By doing so, you will become a far more powerful advocate for your clients.

The essential point of direct is to create a connection between the witness and the jury from which the jurors get to know the witness and the relevant facts of the case through the witness' eyes. The general goals are to:

1. Introduce and validate the witness.
2. Establish (or rebut) a prima facie case of all applicable elements for the record.
3. Paint a dramatic and persuasive picture of the primary facts.
4. Introduce all appropriate documentary and other evidence.

The selection (in those cases where you have a choice) and ordering of witnesses involves a number of strategic choices. The primary consideration is which witness has what information. However, the personality of a witness, in terms of credibility, likeability, and strength to withstand cross-examination, are also important factors. Use logical sequencing, including:

- fact witnesses before experts;
- liability witnesses before damages;

- where possible, sandwich weaker witnesses between stronger ones;
- start strong and end strong;
- be organized and prepared.

I. Getting Organized: The Witness Notebook

The purposes of a good witness notebook, featuring a careful witness outline, are what I call the "3 Cs": Confidence, Control, and Credibility.

Confidence

Knowing that you are well prepared and organized helps overcome some of your natural nervousness. The knowledge that you are prepared assures you that you have minimized the number of surprises and have equipped yourself for those that will inevitably arise.

Control

Eliminates groping, fumbling, and other problems that can distract you (and the jury) from your primary focus. When you have command of the materials and the facts, you have command of the courtroom.

Credibility

With the witness, who will have the confidence that you are on top of things; with the judge, who may be more inclined to rule for you if you clearly know what you are talking about; and with the jury, who will become more inclined to trust and believe you.

To prepare a direct examination, you must broaden your perspective and think creatively. At the risk of sounding corny, I tell people that in order to be in command on direct examination, you should use the BOSS method: Brainstorm, Organize, Storytell, and Simplify.

Brainstorm

Think openly and creatively—alone, with you client, and with others—about who your witness is and what he or she has to offer. The questions for brainstorming include:

- What is *good* about the witness?
- What is *bad* about the witness?
- What *image* do you want the jury to have?
- What did the witness do?
- What does the witness know about the case?

• What does the witness know about other witnesses?

As an aid in this process, see Witness Analysis, Form 12–2.

Organize

Refer to your core documents. Create working files for each witness at the earliest possible moment, and put notes, documents, or anything relevant to that witness in the file as you progress. Mark up copies of your case outline and chronology with who is the best witness to introduce which facts or exhibits, and put those notes in the witness files. Meanwhile, as you review each witness, update the core documents with any new information. Begin your draft witness outline early. (see Checklist for Conducting Examination, Form 12–4.

Storytell

Your witness has to tell—and teach—his or her story to strangers. To help prepare properly, you should do the same. Use others—preferably nonlawyers—to talk to about the witness, the witness's story, and any problems or gaps. Listen to their reactions and questions, and anticipate similar reactions from the jury by putting your best responses into the witness outline.

Simplify

One common danger of all this effort and preparation is that you will lose sight of what is important and *over*-tell the story. In doing so, you may overwhelm the jury with the detail and lose their attention. So, after you have created a witness outline that includes everything, go back and eliminate detail. Simplify the presentation so you focus on the key issues.

II. Witness Outline

It is critical to have a standard format for a witness outline that you are comfortable with and stick to faithfully. You may make your own changes as you go along, but start with a basic system like the one here. Word processing makes developing an outline much easier, but the basic format remains the same whether it is typed or handwritten.Use Form 12–1 (page 210) as a reference for the discussion below.

The first key to a good witness outline is to keep it simple and well spaced. Thus, there should only be one limited topic per page. Caption each page with the name of the witness, and a numbered topic heading with tabs between each topic. The numbered topic heading should then be tied into a table of contents for the whole outline. Being organized does not mean you cannot be flexible: for example, you can always add topics on the spot by inserting a new number or rearrange the order.

Next, draw a line down the page two-thirds of the way over to the right. The larger, left-hand side is for your question notes. The smaller, right-hand side is for annotations and other notes to yourself. Keep to that division faithfully, and eventually it will become comfortable and routine.

The question notes on the left-hand side should be widely spaced and set off with bullets. The more you write, the more you will read, so your notes should only be one or two word reminders. What key words will keep you on track? The exceptions to this format are foundational or hypothetical questions that you may want to have more carefully written out.

The right side annotations are most often in one of the four categories shown in the sample page at Form 12–1.

Prior Statements

Include any type of prior statement by the witness, from transcribed testimony (such as deposition, as referenced in the appendix), to a statement taken by an investigator. The note should include a precise reference (for example, to page and line.)

Documents

Use either the exhibit number (as in the appendix) or, if it is not yet an exhibit, some other identifier as a reference. If the document is a multiple-page text, also reference the page and paragraph or line.

Legal Cites

If the question references some type of legal requirement, prohibition, or whatever, the precise citation should be included.

Procedural Notes

In the craziness of trial, lawyers often forget to do some of the most basic things. One good example is to *offer* an exhibit into evidence once it has been properly identified and authenticated. Here is a good place to put reminders of some of those basic procedural steps.

The next step is to draw a line across the page about two inches from the bottom. The space below that line is to anticipate objections on this topic, whether to the admissibility of a document (as in Form 12–1), the relevancy of an issue, or other types of problems. When you know that admissibility of an important item may be contested, you may wish to file a motion in limine before trial to get the judge to resolve it. If not, you may want to have a minimemo, no more than one or two pages, ready to use as a reference, and hand to the court. The motion or memo can be referenced and summarized here, or just the key point and key cite.

Finally, any document that is important enough to reference in either the right side annotations or the bottom notes should be *in* the Witness Notebook, right after the topic page. Each document should be included in two forms: first, a copy of the relevant page 3-hole punched into the binder, and with the key words highlighted for your easy reference. Second, a clean copy of the full document (in a 3-hole punched plastic pocket), so it can be easily removed and handed to the witness. Depending on the court and the situation, you may need *several* clean copies: for opposing counsel and the court. If the document you are referencing is a lengthy one (for example, a deposition transcript) be sure to have the full transcript readily available, but you may want to consider putting clean copies of only the cover page and relevant transcript page(s) in the notebook.

III. Effective Direct

Nonleading Questions

Leading questions are simply questions that contain part of the answer. The general rule against using them on direct (see, for example, FRE 611(c)) is an extraordinarily difficult stumbling block for many lawyers and, as a result, the object of much disdain. Yet it should not be viewed so negatively for two reasons: first, because it is one of those rare technical rules that actually makes enormous substantive sense; second, because with guidance, practice, and discipline, it is not that hard to follow the rule.

On the first point, think of the rule against leading questions as an opportunity, not an obstacle. The challenge of direct examination is to have the *witness* tell his or her story to the jury, while the lawyer exercises control without appearing to do so. The rule against leading questions helps this process in several ways.

1. It emphasizes that it is the witness's testimony, not the lawyer's. It pushes the witness to the forefront, and helps the lawyer to disappear into the background, encouraging the very important direct link between the witness and the jury.
2. It helps avoid conversational shorthand. If both the lawyer and the witness know the case well, they will both tend to talk in shorthand: presuming knowledge of much of the background and explanations,

and skipping quickly to where they want to go. If the lawyer is asking leading questions, that only accelerates the process. Meanwhile, the jury is alienated and lost. Asking nonleading questions forces you to slow down, take things step by step, and ask for the basic information that might be skipped over in a fast exchange.

3. Asking nonleading questions forces you to listen more carefully to the witness's words, not your own. Has he or she explained something fully? What else is there? How do I ask for more? By slowing down the process, you can focus on the most effective possible direct examination.

On the second point, asking nonleading questions is manageable if you just keep it simple. Think about it: if a leading question contains both question and answer, what would a nonleading question have to be? Shorter and simpler.

- Shorter is easy to do. Be mechanical about it. Aside from language that is transitional ("directing your attention to the morning of April 3, . . .") or foundational ("is this record made and kept in the ordinary course of business . . ."), if a question on direct examination is more than three or four words long, it is probably leading. A red flag should go up in your mind. Moreover, leading or not, why are you asking a long question on direct? *Don't do it.* Break the questioning up into individual parts.

- Simpler can also be accomplished—simply. The essence of direct examination is to prompt the witness to the next subject or the appropriate qualifier. For subject, use the famous litany of "who, what, when, why, where." For qualifiers, use easy ones like "else" and "next." 90 percent or more of direct examination can be conducted with these simple words. For the times when you get stuck, just commit them to memory as a simple grid:

Subject	Qualifier	Example
Who		Who else was there?
What		What happened next?
When	Else	When did you see him next?
Why	Next	Why else did you do that?
Where		Where else were they?

Having tried to emphasize that asking nonleading questions is manageable, let me add one qualifier. The discipline of the rule against leading questions is unnatural and difficult for many lawyers. Without adequate preparation, it can be even more unnatural and difficult for the witness. Lawyers they have seen on TV *always* ask outrageous leading questions. You need to make sure the witness understands the rule, and that the burden is on them to tell their story. Stress that they should listen very carefully to your prompt in the question. If you say "else," it probably means that there *is* something else, and they should try hard to remember. If you say "next," it likewise probably means they have not finished.

Foundations

One key exception to the rule against leading questions on direct, and therefore an important issue for preparation, involves questions that provide a required legal foundation. There are many of these, but some of the more common include:

1. Business Records (see, for example, FRE Rule 803(6));
2. Character Evidence (see, for example, FRE Rule 405); and
3. Expert Testimony (hypotheticals, and so forth) (see, for example, FRE Rule 703).

Since much of this sounds like mumbo jumbo to the unprepared layperson, be sure to prepare your witness, and your jury, for these kinds of legalistic questions.

Refreshing Recollection

No matter how good a witness may be, and no matter how well prepared, people forget things. People under stress, such as being in the witness box, forget even more. Knowing this, it is essential that both you and your witness be prepared. You and your witness can avoid the problems associated with forgetting by following some simple rules.

1. <u>Never say never</u>. If a witness forgets something, you can generally only help him if he leaves the door open to be helped. In other words, if a witness makes an absolute statement (*yes, no, never, none*), there is no basis to refresh his recollection, because he has not indicated any lack of memory. Prepare your witnesses to "never say never": only be as absolute as he or she is absolutely sure. Otherwise, leave the door open by saying "that's all I can remember" or words to that effect.

2. <u>Listen carefully.</u> If a witness has forgotten something but does not realize it, it is up to the lawyer to prompt, and the witness to respond. Ask the witness if there is anything else. If that does not work, try asking if he or she is sure there isn't anything else. Hopefully, at some point, and with the right preparation, the witness will get the hint.

3. <u>Refreshing recollection with questions.</u> Once the witness makes clear that he or she has exhausted his or her memory, the lawyer may wish to try to refresh recollection with questions. First, you may want to just ask the question again, or with some other qualifiers ("Now, take your time, and tell us . . .", "think hard for a minute, was . . ."). Failing that, if lack of memory is clear, many courts will give you some latitude to ask leading questions. (for example, "Was Jane Smith at that meeting?").

4. <u>Refreshing recollection with documents or objects.</u> Virtually anything can refresh memory, although the most common approach involves documents or prior statements. The key is that you are refreshing recollection, not creating or substituting for it. Does what you show the witness cause her to remember what she had previously forgotten? When you use objects to refresh memory, you must follow a general protocol:

   a. Get the witness to say his or her memory is exhausted.

   b. Show the witness the documents (in many courts, you should simultaneously show it to the court and counsel) (see, FRE Rule 612).

   c. Have the witness read the document to him or herself, then put it aside (so the witness is clearly testifying from memory, not reading); and

   d. Ask the witness if looking at the document refreshed his or her memory;

   e. Ask the witness what he or she now remembers.

5. <u>Past recollection recorded.</u> If you are unable to refresh the witness's memory, but there is a prior document that accurately reflects the facts responsive to the question, you may be able to get those prior statements before the jury as Past Recollection Recorded (see, FRE Rule 803(5)). In this way, the previous statement is substituted for current memory (although the document itself cannot usually be admitted).

Documentary Evidence and Exhibits

There are two objectives in presenting documentary evidence and exhibits: 1) to supplement, corroborate, or clarify witness testimony, and 2) to attack the objectivity, accuracy, or completeness of the adverse party's exhibits. In all cases the evidence should be pertinent to the issues and clear and easy for the jury to understand.

Clarify and simplify your exhibits. Summarize voluminous records where their volume or bulk makes them unmanageable or unintelligible to the jury or where there are numerous custodians. This may be allowed when the summarizer is available as witness, and the originals were available for inspection before trial. Obtain stipulations of admissibility whenever possible.

Plan your presentation of exhibits for maximum effect. Consider using photo enlargements or an overhead projector for documents and/or exhibits that are an integral part of your chain of proof or that will be referred to or marked by more than one witness.

Keep in mind your strategy in using documents and exhibits. Introduce them with a witness who can add to the narrative or explain the document. Refer to portions or contents in your questions to the witness. Use documents and exhibits as opportunities, not obstacles: they are a supplement to actual testimony, not a substitute. Generally, have the witness testify about the subject matter and even the document *before* you actually give it to him or her. Then, give it to the witness and have him or her identify, offer, and explain it. This sequence ensures a full presentation of the facts, and highlights the document's substance and importance.

Once in court, carefully plan out the logistics of working with documents and exhibits, always keeping in mind Murphy's Law, that if something can go wrong, it will go wrong. Among the questions to consider:

- What equipment do you need (easels, projectors, pointers);
- How are you going to get everything to court;
- Is it organized so that you can easily put your fingers on what you need;
- Is each witness comfortable and familiar with everything you (or opposing counsel) are going to show or give her;
- If something is to be read, you read it, then get the witness to confirm;
- Listen carefully to make sure both you and the witness clearly identify exhibits and documents, so that the record does not end up with unidentifiable "this," "that," and "there."

See Form 12–6, Checklist for Introduction of Documentary Evidence and Exhibits.

Demonstrative Evidence

Any visual exhibit that assists the judge or jury in understanding the proof or testimony on the issues is demonstrative evidence. Since psychological tests show that after three days, persons of average intelligence will remember 65 percent of what they have seen and heard—as opposed to 10 percent of what they have just heard without visual evidence—the use of demonstrative evidence may provide an edge of 55 percent in establishing your proof to the trier of fact.

Illustrating medical testimony using anatomical models and charts is one of the more dramatic and familiar uses of demonstrative evidence. Other types of demonstrative evidence are:

1. Charts and graphs.
2. Drawings, illustrations, X-rays.
3. Photographs, videotapes, motion pictures.
4. Maps, diagrams, surveys.
5. Models.
6. Mock-ups, experiments, tests.
7. Chronologies, calendars, and so forth.
8. Any other objects or real evidence.

Here again, remember that demonstrative evidence is intended to complement and support your witnesses, not to replace them. Use only evidence or exhibits that will clearly and dramatically depict important points to the jury. Do not overwhelm the jury with a dazzling array of visual aids that will distract them from the witnesses' testimony. See Form 12–7, Checklist for Using Demonstrative Evidence.

Objections

Objections to your examination are inevitable but need not be a problem. Treat them as opportunities, not obstacles, and you will impress the jury and silence your opponents. For example:

- Anticipate objections. As you prepare your examination, think about what questions or testimony might be subject to objection, and prepare a concise response. As noted above, use the bottom of the page on the witness outline to quote applicable evidentiary rules or case law. Prepare your witnesses for these and other objectives.
- Never let objections bother and distract you. Brush them off and keep going.
- If the objection is overruled, take the opportunity to restate the question (or have the court reporter read it back) to refocus the witness and emphasize the interruption.

- If the objection is sustained, do not get off track. Most objections go to the form of your question, not the subject matter. Use the objection as an opportunity to break the question up into its parts, or ask it in a better form.
- If the objection is sustained on the subject matter, consider going to sidebar to argue the point or make an offer of proof for the record. There may also be alternative theories of admissibility.
- Always have a fall back question ready when an objection is sustained; do not give up. See Checklist for Making for Objections and Excluding Evidence, Form 12–8.

V. Preparing Witnesses for Direct

Logistics

No matter how much TV a witness has watched, real courtrooms and court procedures are foreign territory to most people. Explain and walk your witness through each step of the way. Take him or her to see the courtroom, if feasible, or at least map it out and practice as if you were in court.

Do not allow witnesses to be in the presence of the jury prior or subsequent to the time of their testimony. This means that witnesses should be scheduled quite accurately and be absent from the courthouse other than when they are called. A carefully dressed thirteen-year-old girl who testified beautifully and then appears after lunch in the hallway with dangling earrings and smacking chewing gum (both typical thirteen-year-old behaviors) may well give the jury the idea that they did not see "the real thing."

It should be the lawyer's goal to make the space of the courtroom work for the witnesses. If direct examination can best be conducted in some way other than the traditional manner, do it. Be certain to explain the purposes and reasons for any unusual method of examination during your opening statement. If the witness will be doing a demonstration for the jury, it might be best for him or her to sit facing them. A very young child may be more comfortable on the witness stand if held by his or her mother, a social worker, or in special cases, the lawyer. Whatever way the witness is presented should demonstrate to the jurors that these witnesses are real people who are telling a real story.

When the witness does testify from the witness stand, your positioning should spotlight attention on the witness and not on the questioner. Standing at the far end of the jury box is one position that accomplishes this. It encourages the witness to speak clearly and loudly enough for the entire jury. It allows the lawyer to watch the response of the jurors without being watched by them.

Question and Answer Communication

The most important part of witness preparation is helping people learn to communicate in the question and answer format. It is an unnatural and difficult process for most people. A full discussion of witness preparation is beyond the scope of this book (see, *Preparing Witnesses: A Practical Guide for Lawyers and Their Clients*, Daniel I. Small, Chicago: ABA,1998). However, there are some key rules for witnesses direct examination that are worth emphasizing here:

1. Listen carefully. Since the lawyer generally cannot ask leading questions, the witness has to listen carefully to what is really being asked, and listen particularly carefully for the kind of prompts discussed above.

2. Take your time. Listening and responding thoughtfully and carefully takes time. Slow down.

3. Respond fully. The general rule for witnesses is: don't volunteer. Answer the precise question and stop. However, in some circumstances on Direct, because the lawyer cannot ask leading questions, you may want to prepare the witness to use your questions as a starting point, but then to take more of the responsibility to tell the detailed story.

4. Tell the truth. Don't say what you think someone wants you to say: just say the truth. If you are asked what counsel told you to say, the easiest and best answer is "the truth."

5. Do not answer a question you don't understand. Just ask the questioner to ask it again or rephrase it.

6. If you do not remember, say so. Never worry about not remembering, and don't be absolute ("yes, no, none, never") when the truth is that you don't remember absolutely. Just say "I don't remember" or "that's all I remember right now."

7. Do not guess. This means avoid guessing as to factual details (dates, numbers, and so forth) and also with inferences, conclusions, opinions (could have, should have, would have, must have).

8. Keep it simple. Avoid jargon or fancy speech, and generally limit your answer to the question asked.

9. <u>Be careful with documents.</u> Take the time to look them over carefully and make sure that you—and the jury—understand what you are looking at.

10. <u>Use your counsel.</u> Listen for questions that are prompts ("what else . . ." "are you sure. . ."). Also, if there are objections, don't get involved in any back and forth exchanges, but listen carefully. It can help you understand what direction the questioning will take.

Further Reading

Murray, Peter. *Basic Trial Advocacy*. Boston: Little, Brown and Company, 1995.

Sandler, Paul Mark. *Model Witness Examinations*, Chicago: ABA, 1997.

Small, Daniel I. *Preparing Witnesses: A Practical Guide for Lawyers and Their Clients*. Chicago: ABA, 1998.

12-1 SAMPLE WITNESS OUTLINE

CAPT. SMITH

5. SHIP'S LOG

<u>1990—Captain: Flying Dove</u>	(Depo., p. 187, 1.6)
Fishing Grand Banks	
Responsible: ship's documents	
<u>Log—Important</u>	
Required by Coast Guard	(38 C.F.R. 1089)
—Captain Responsible	
Records tip	
<u>Flying Dove Log</u>	(Exhibit 37)
—Handwriting	
—Accurate	—Offer (Exh. 37, p. 38)
—Feb. 3, 1990	

Bismark v. Titanic, 508 F.2d 193, 198 (1st Cir., 1991) ("Commercial ship's log is a business record if kept in the ordinary course. . . .")

12-2 WITNESS ANALYSIS

For: __ Client

Name of Witness: _____   __ Opponent

Home Address: _____   Home Phone: _____

Employer: _____   Work Phone: _____

Employer's Address: _____   Occupation: _____

__ Expert: __ Medical? Field of expertise: _____

__ If expert, summary of qualifications:

_____

__ Adverse Witness?   __Call under MRE/FRE 611(c) as adverse party?

_____

_____

Client Expects Witness to Prove:

—   _____

—   _____

—   _____

—   _____

—   _____

—   _____

—   _____

—   _____

Basis for Impeaching Witness:

—   _____

—   _____

—   _____

—   _____

—   _____

—   _____

—   _____

__ Request statement or report.   __Statement or report obtained on _____

     by _____   Does opponent have copy? __Yes __No

     __Attached   __Filed: _____

__ Schedule Deposition __Deposition subpoena issued. __Duces Tecum.
__ Deposition taken on _____ __ Transcript received.
__ Reviewed testimony with witness on _____ Appearance?_____
Cooperative?_____ Believable?_____ Demeanor? _____
Reliable? _____ Other observations: _____
__ Subpoena for trial necessary __Duces Tecum __Subpoena Letter
__ Prepared __ Issued Serving Officer: _____, __ Served

Points to Be Covered by Trial

__ _____

__ _____

__ _____

__ _____

__ _____

__ _____

__ _____

__ _____

_____

12-3 EXHIBIT ANALYSIS

Nature of Exhibit: _____ __ Copy Attached

Date: _____ Exhibit for ____ Client   __ Opponent

Prepared by: _____ __Witness Analysis Prepared

Obtained from: _____ __Witness Analysis Prepared

Original with: _____ __Witness Analysis Prepared

_____

_____

__ Complaint   __ Counterclaim   __ Reply
                                                    Exhibit No.: _____
__ Answer   __ Cross-claim   __ 3rd Party Claim

Preliminary Examination Exhibit No.: ___   Transcript, pp. _____

__ Plaintiff's Deposition Exhibit No.: ____   See Transcript pp. _____

__ Defendant's Deposition Exhibit No.:   See Transcript pp. _____

__ See Transcript of Deposition of _____, pp. _____

__ See Transcript of Deposition of _____, pp. _____

__ See Transcript of Deposition of _____, pp. _____

Trial Exhibit: __Plaintiff   Defendant Exhibit No.:_____   __ Admitted

_____

_____

Exhibit Submitted to Establish: _____
_____
_____

Grounds for Objection: _____
_____
_____

Client's Position: _____
_____
_____

Other Witnesses or Exhibit to Support Client's Position: _____
_____
_____

__ Analysis Form Completed

_____

Related Exhibits
__ Analysis Form Completed

— _____
— _____
— _____
— _____
— _____
— _____
— _____

Client: _____ Matter: _____

12-4 CHECKLIST FOR CONDUCTING EXAMINATION OF A LAY WITNESS

A. General rules.

   1. Write notes for each witness.

   2. Prepare general questions to allow witness to tell story "in his own way."

   3. Use well-spaced questions to avoid objections to witness's narrative and, only if necessary, interruptions that will:
       a. Keep witness on point.
       b. Draw out evidence omitted.
       c. Qualify a broad statement.
       d. Amplify a vague statement.
       e. Clarify ambiguity.
       f. Emphasize important points.

   4. Avoid repetition.

   5. Minimize harmful evidence by introducing with whatever explanation is available, and anticipate introduction by adversary.
       a. Discuss in jury voir dire, and then let defendant bring upon cross-exam, particularly if explainable.
       b. Explain in redirect—sympathetic circumstances, remoteness, subsequent position of trust, restoration of community reputation.

   6. Evidence of questionable admissibility. use if persuasive value outweighs chance of reversal.

   7. Prove oral statements. (See Objections—Hearsay, in Checklist for Making Objections and Excluding Evidence).

   8. Offer for limited purpose—impeaching statement not adopted by offering party.

   9. Don't press witness on omissions or errors; return later and refresh recollection.

B. Refreshing witness memory.

   1. Request recess to calm nervous witness.

   2. Use leading questions to direct attention to subject matter.

3. Present refreshed recollection.
   a. Material thing—whatever it is and without limitation as to evidence or admission—may be shown to witness if may help remember.
   b. Witness then testifies from memory.

4. If recollection not refreshed, introduce document as past recollection that was recorded.
   a. Establish witness's familiarity with facts in general.
   b. Establish that he or she knew facts in past.
   c. Establish that he or she doesn't now remember.
   d. Either establish document in evidence or prepared by witness or under his or her direction.
   e. Establish that document was accurately made at time of event or while facts fresh in mind.

C. Proving telephone conversation—foundation.

1. Witness originated call to person he or she did not know.
   a. Called number listed in directory under _____.
   b. Asked for person by name, title, or description.
   c. Person who answered identified self as person called.
   d. Person discussed matters connected with firm called.

2. Witness received call from person he or she did not know.
   a. Identity established by subject matter of conversation.
   b. Caller identified subsequently.
      1) Circumstances of original call.
      2) Subsequent occasions to speak to caller.
      3) Subsequent familiarity with caller's voice.
      4) Recognition of caller's voice in original call.

3. Identification of caller's voice in pretrial exam or courtroom.

D. Handwriting—nonexpert:

1. Is witness acquainted with handwriting of the person?

2. Circumstances of seeing handwriting.
   a. Correspondence.
   b. Familiarity through business contact.

3. Is this handwriting of person?

E. Plaintiff's testimony on injuries and damages.

    1. Utilize plaintiff's medical and expense diary.

    2. Describe pain and suffering—complaints.
       a. Nontreating medical expert cannot testify to description of pain and suffering. Unless obtained from plaintiff, it is hearsay.
       b. Visits to doctor—number and frequency.
       c. Hospitalizations.

F. Adverse party as first witness under cross-exam.

    1. Advantages and strategy.
       a. Use leading questions.
       b. May impeach.
       c. Establish scope as broad as pleadings. Direct by own counsel limited to material on cross-exam.
       d. Commit defendant to a position on issues, or gain admissions before defendant hears your case.
       e. Use party's deposition rather than calling to stand.

    2. Disadvantages.
       a. First impression to jury is defendant's version.
       b. You have no control over what may be said.

G. Impeachment of own witness.

    1. Traditional—Use earlier contradictory statements.

    2. Credibility of witness may be attacked by any party under federal rules.

    3. Strategy—Attack directly or collaterally by other witnesses?
       a. Use tactic that clearly and forcefully defeats witness.
       b. Use prior contradictory statement immediately and later use witnesses to further disprove.

H. Failure to call witness—unfavorable inference.

    1. Exceptions.
       a. Merely cumulative corroborative witness. Failure to corroborate party—not within exception.
       b. Witness equally available to both parties.
          1) Hostile or adverse witness not equally available.

   2) Factors of availability.
      a) Party's knowledge of identity.
      b) Witness's probable testimony.
      c) Relationship and control between party and witness.

2. Explain absence—no presumption: Illness, death, removal from jurisdiction.

3. Obtain witness's evidence prior to trial.
   a. Request stipulation of defendant's witnesses—on refusal, argue presumption.
   b. Preserve your witness's testimony by deposition prior to trial.

4. Cover presumption in final argument and instructions.

I. Sequestration of witnesses.

12-5 PREPARATION AND EXAMINATION OF EXPERT WITNESS—GENERAL CHECKLIST

A. General use of expert.

    1. Investigation.

    2. Determining issues and drafting pleadings.

    3. Settlement.

    4. Trial.

B. Selection criteria.

    1. Ability to communicate to jury.
        a. Simplify technical language.
        b. Talk on layperson's level.

    2. Vulnerability to cross-exam.
        a. Prior published contrary views.
        b. Lacks up-to-date knowledge.

    3 Experience as witness.
        a. Avoid one who always appears on same side.
        b. Generally, avoid someone with no witness experience.

    4. Determine opinions prior to retention.
        a. Informal review and discussions.
        b. Federal rules allow opposing party to discover retained expert's opinions.

C. Preparation of expert testimony.

    1. Establish comprehensive overview of case and expert's role in proof.

    2. Establish how tests and experiments conducted.

    3. Review opposing expert's reports and opinions.

    4. Avoid advocacy position.

    5. Complete qualification checklist.
        a. Date and state of license.
        b. Education—schools and degrees.
        c. Specialized training.

       d.   Description of specialty.

       e.   Experience, including military service—time and type.

       f.   Industry, company, or institutional affiliations.

       g.   Association and society memberships.

       h.   Publications and familiarity with literature in field.

       i.   Professional honors.

6.   Jury Relations. Speak to jurors and explain technical terms.

7.   Request a list of reading material in field from expert.

D. Hypothetical questions.

1.   Types.
    a.   Opinion based on first-hand observation and evidence heard. Use in nonjury trial or in simple fact situations.
    b.   Opinion based on narrative statement of evidence presented. Better form—summarize and emphasize important points.
    c.   Opinion on out-of-court data and hearsay evidence.
       1)   Requires no hypothetical foundation.
       2)   Discovery—interrogatories to learn facts.

2.   Narrative hypothetical question—structure.
    a.   Establish fact history.
    b.   Establish performance of acts complained of.
       1)   Omit evidence admitted over objection unless necessary to opinion.
       2)   Omit sharply disputed evidence unless necessary.
       3)   Each fact to be assumed must already be in evidence. The judge can waive this requirement upon showing good cause and counsel's assurance that it will be put into evidence before the close of the case.
    c.   Establish opinion on causation and deviation from standard.

3.   Drafting the hypothetical question.
    a.   Make it persuasive but honest—simple and clear.
    b.   Review with expert for suggestions.

4.   The question—an example.
    a.   First state every relevant element of your case as specifically as possible; then present questions.
    b.   "Have we discussed these facts previously as well as your conclusions based upon them?" (This allows the jury to know that this is

a *considered* opinion coming up, to a spur-of-the-moment reaction.)

    c.   "Assuming all of the facts I have stated are true . . ." or

    d.   "Based on the facts you have stated to the jury, do you have an opinion as to what caused the traumatic injuries to the brain that the child suffered on the ____/____/____ and, further, as to what caused his death on ____/____/____?" or

    e.   "Based on a reasonable certainty and on your experience as a surgeon in a Montana community of 5,000 people approximately 300 miles from a medical center with physicians of more specialized practice, do you have an opinion as to whether the course pursued by the operating surgeon was such a course as could responsibly be pursued by a skillful, careful, and competent practitioner engaged in the surgery in the similarly situated community of on ____/____/____?"

    f.   "And what is that opinion?" (N.B. See Rule 58 of the Uniform Rules of Evidence. Questions calling for an expert opinion need no longer be hypothetical in nature.)

E.   Learned treatises. Use in direct exam.

    1.   Admissibility (check jurisdiction).
        a.   Federal rules allow reading into evidence.
        b.   Foundation is required.

    2.   Strategy considerations.
        a.   Anticipate attack on opinions and bolster authorities in advance for rebuttal or redirect.
        b.   Avoid if exposure to damaging cross-exam.

F.   Court-appointed expert.

    1.   Decision to appoint—considerations.
        a.   Need to appoint expert versus impact on jury.
        b.   Need to break settlement stalemate.
        c.   Need to identify technical issues in ending dispute.
        d.   Need to obtain reluctant experts in controversial cases.

    2.   Instructions to expert.
        a.   Cover testing methods, authorities, treatises.
        b.   Evaluate other expert's opinions.

12-6 CHECKLIST FOR INTRODUCTION OF DOCUMENTARY EVIDENCE AND EXHIBITS

A. Introduction into evidence.

1. Mark for identification.

2. Have witness identify—recognize it and tell what it is.

3. Lay foundation. (See sec. B. below.)

4. Show it to opposing counsel, who has right to examine only when offered in evidence. If document identified on cross-exam of your witness, keep your witness available to explain if later offered.

5. Offer into evidence.

6. Obtain court ruling on admission.

7. Show or read exhibit to judge or jury.

B. Foundation for admission.

1. General.
    a. Authenticity. Is it what it purports to be?
    b. Relevance. Does it apply to fact issue in case?

2. Business records (check local rules).
    a. Was information transmitted by someone in business with knowledge?
    b. Is witness custodian or maker?
    c. Are records kept in regular course of business?
    d. Are records customarily made close in time to events recorded?
    e. Was exhibit made in above customary procedure?
    f. Examples:
        1) Hospital records (excluding history and hearsay).
        2) Police records—in civil cases where informant in police business.
        3) Deceased doctor's reports.
        4) Weather reports.
        5) Autopsy and lab reports.

3. Official and public records. No foundation required.

4. Past recollection recorded.

    a.   Notes and memos made by witness may be introduced if recollection not refreshed and proper foundation laid (see VIII. B. above).

    b.   Federal rules include records "adopted" by witness.

5. Best evidence rule.
    a.   Duplicates admissible unless:
       1) Genuine question of authenticity of original.
       2) Unfair to admit duplicate under circumstances existing at time of trial.
    b.   Other evidence of contents allowed if witness is familiar with contents or if original is:
       1) Lost or destroyed and search made.
       2) Not obtainable.
       3) In opponent's possession.
       4) Concerns collateral matter.

6. Authorities, texts, standards, and scientific data.
    a.   Recognized as authoritative.
    b.   Authored by witness.

7. Writings not authored or witnessed by witness.
    a.   Received in mail and contents indicate it is answer to letter by witness.
    b.   Subsequently acknowledged by author.
    c.   Handwriting expert opinion.

12-7 CHECKLIST FOR USING DEMONSTRATIVE EVIDENCE

A. Charts and graphs.

1. Uses.
    a. To compare economic material.
    b. To show complex human relationships, organizational structures.
    c. To show time and events.

2. Method.
    a. Single chart (simple figures) or several (complex).
    b. Different colors or shapes.
    c. Graphs or calendars with events marked on plastic overlays.

B. Illustrations and X-rays.

1. Medical illustrations to complement X-rays and show soft-tissue injuries. Use plastic overlays to show progression of injury and damage.

2. Positive X-rays.

C. Photographs.

1. Use—investigation, preservation of evidence, preparation of witnesses, trial.

2. Admissibility.
    a. Foundation—fair and accurate representation of subject in a given photo taken.
    b. Factors in preparing and attacking photos.
        1) Normal lens used? Wide-angle and telephoto cause distortions.
        2) Height camera held? Was it eye level?
        3) Black-and-white photos don't distinguish old and new damages; high quality color photos do. Avoid instant development color prints if possible.
        4) Skid marks—Use ruler or tape in photo.
        5) Skid marks—Photograph with sun behind and from center of marks.
        6) Illumination of subject affected by exposure and developing time.
        7) Proper viewing distance—focal length and enlargement factor of negative to print.

3. Trial use.
   a. Enlargement on easel.
   b. Overhead projector and slides.
   c. Photos marked with colored crayons.
   d. 3-D photos.

4. Motion pictures—uses.
   a. Shows movement or speed.
   b. Shows sequence of events or acts—"day in life."
   c. Shows operation of machinery or other evidence not otherwise available in court.
   d. Admissibility. It is relevant, accurate, and will assist the jury.
      1) Take evidence as to speed and lighting so can compare with projection speed.
      2) If edited, how was it done, by whom, and what is difference from original?

D. Maps, diagrams, and surveys.

1. Use to depict relationship of physical characteristics of area or general system.
   a. Give specific instructions to maker.
   b. Tape to magnetic board in court.
   c. Mark objects on map as told by witness or shown on photo for record.
   d. Use overlays.

2. Admissibility.
   a. Relevant to fact issues in dispute.
   b. Witness testimony to scale and accuracy.

E. Models (admissibility same as maps).

1. Scene—good for overview to complement photos and maps.

2. Anatomical—medical.

3. Operational—used only with care and extensive preparation and pre-trial testing.

F. Experiments and tests made under conditions and circumstances similar to those existing at time of accident.

G. Computer printouts.

1. Use.
   a. Search, analysis, negative records.
   b. Simulation of auto accident program.

2. Foundation requirements.
   a. Computer was correctly programmed and regularly produces same kind of material.
   b. Base input data is systematically prepared from admissible information.
   c. There is no reasonable cause to suspect departure from system or error in preparation of data.
   d. There was no malfunction by computer.
   e. There were no alterations to mechanism or computer process or no records kept of alterations made.
   f. There is no cause to believe accuracy or validity has been adversely affected by improper process, procedure, or safeguards.

H. Real evidence foundation.

1. Object is unique; only one so it is admitted as real thing.

2. Object is not naturally unique, but witness did something to it that makes it unique, for example, initials.

3. Object is not unique and not altered; proof of chain of custody is necessary.

4. Object is offered not as the unique item, but as one similar to or consistent with the unique item.

12-8 CHECKLIST FOR MAKING OBJECTIONS AND EXCLUDING EVIDENCE

I. Types of Objections

A. Objections to witnesses—competency.

 1. Judge sitting on case not competent as witness.

 2. Juror on case not competent except as to:
    a. Extraneous prejudicial information improperly before jury.
    b. Outside influence on juror.

 3. See local law re:
    a. Minors.
    b. Spouses.
    c. Mental condition.
    d. Dead man's statute.

B. Objections to evidence.

 1. Irrelevant—not probative of issue or not proving a fact of consequence to the issue.
    a. Unfairly prejudicial—gruesome picture to improperly and emotionally influence jurors.
    b. Confusion of issues.
    c. Misleading jury.
    d. Undue delay.
    e. Needless cumulative evidence.
    f. Character evidence—not relevant to show action in conformity with character. Exceptions:
       1) Pertinent character trait offered by accused or on rebuttal by prosecution.
       2) Character of victim of crime, except victim's past sexual behavior in rape case.
       3) Character of witness for untruthfulness, if evidence of untruthfulness may then introduce truthfulness.
       4) Impeachment.
       5) Other crimes or acts.
          a) Not admissible to show character of person and action in conformance therewith.
          b) Admissible for motive, opportunity, intent, preparation, knowledge, identify absence of mistake, or accident.

6) Insurance, when used to show negligent or wrongful act; okay to show ownership or control.

7) Settlement or plea offer or discussions.

2. Hearsay—an out-of-court statement offered to prove the truth of the matter asserted.
   a. Not hearsay.
      1) Prior inconsistent statements.
      2) Prior statement for rebuttal.
      3) Statement of prior identification of person.
      4) Admission by party opponent.
      5) Demonstrating knowledge of fact or person.
      6) Demonstrating falsity of statements or document.
      7) Demonstrating notice.
      8) Demonstrating state of mind.
   b. Exceptions to hearsay where availability of declarant immaterial.
      1) Present sense impression.
      2) Excited utterance.
      3) Then existing mental, emotional, and physical condition.
      4) Statements for purpose of medical diagnostic treatment.
      5) Recorded recollection (where witness once had knowledge but now has insufficient recollection).
      6) Records of regularly conducted activities (business records).
      7) Public records and reports.
      8) Record of vital statistics.
   c. Exceptions to hearsay where declarant is unavailable.
      1) Exemption to testify on the grounds of privilege.
      2) Refuse to testify in spite of court order to do so.
      3) Testified as to lack of memory.
      4) Dead or suffering physical or mental illness.
      5) Absent from the hearing and unable to be compelled to attend.
         a) Former testimony (where there was opportunity to develop the testimony by direct cross or redirect examination).
         b) Dying declaration.
            (1) Declarant believed death was imminent when the statement was made.
            (2) Concerning the cause or circumstances of whether defendant declarant believed to be impending death.
         c) Statement against interest (at the time of the statement it was contrary to the declarant's pecuniary proprietary interest, subjected declarant to civil or criminal liability, or rendered invalid claim by declarant against another).

3. Opinion.
   a. Expert witnesses.
      1) Qualified by knowledge, skill, experience, training, education, or otherwise.
      2) May answer hypothetical questions, but hypothetical questions are not required.
      3) May testify on facts made known outside of hearing.
      4) May not instruct on principle of law.
   b. Lay witness: admissible only if rationally based on witness's perception or helpful to the clear understanding of witness's testimony or the determination of fact in issue (owner can testify to value of own property).

4. Lack of foundation.
   a. Business records.
      1) Memorandum or compilation.
      2) Made at or near time.
      3) By or from information transmitted by a person with knowledge.
      4) Kept in regular course of business.
      5) And was a regular practice to make such memorandum or compilation.
   b. Best evidence—original document versus duplicate.
   c. Oral statement.
      1) Fact that statement made.
      2) Identification of speaker.
      3) Identification of persons hearing statement.
      4) Establish time, place, and circumstances.
      5) Ask witness to repeat statement or its substance.
   d. Parole evidence.

5. Privilege and related grounds. Examples:
   a. Attorney-client.
   b. Priest-penitent.
   c. Physician-patient.
   d. Psychologist-patient.
   e. Husband-wife.
   f. Journalist-source.
   g. Informant's identity.
   h. Self-incrimination.
   i. Official information—privacy act.
   j. Trade secret.
   k. Lawyer's work product.

6. Lack of proper foundation for secondary evidence.

7. Nonresponsive answer.

8. Self-serving statements or evidence.

9. Reading from document not in evidence.

10. Conclusions of law or fact.

11. Enlarging pleadings.

C. Objections to form of question.

1. Leading questions—objectionable (three types).
   a. Question calling for yes or no answer—"Was light green at intersection?" Witness not relating a fact to the jury, but lawyer asking if fact he or she wants to establish is true.
   b. Question that suggests answer desired—"What part of crosswalk were you on?" Lawyer's question implies fact of position on crosswalk.
   c. Question that assumes fact in controversy—"Where was plaintiff when defendant went through light at 45 mph?" Lawyer's question is based on facts he or she wishes to prove.

2. Ambiguous.

3. Argumentative.

4. Already answered (redundant).

5. Assumes fact not in evidence.

6. Compound question.

7. Confusing or unintelligible.

8. Improper hypothetical question.

II. Strategy—To Object or Not to Object

A. Purposes of objections.

1. Exclude improper evidence.

2. Preserve point for appeal.

3. Alert judge to area of potentially objectionable testimony.

4. Instruct witness who is under cross-exam.

B. Factors in decision.

    1. Need depends on strengths or weaknesses of case—determine and evaluate specific areas of anticipated objections prior to trial.

    2. Effect on jury of judge sustaining or overruling objections.

    3. Overriding need to save your witness on cross-exam.

C. Overall effect of objections sustained or overruled.

    1. Generally object only when judge will sustain.
        a. Frivolous objection calls jury's attention to evidence.
        b. Frequent objections irritate the jury.

    2. Leading questions. Object if leading form:
        a. Affects accuracy of answer.
        b. Amounts to lawyer testifying.

    3. Inadmissibility of substantive evidence. Object if:
        a. Evidence harmful, objections will be sustained, and admission would not open door to other evidence beneficial to your case.
        b. Evidence harmful and objection will be overruled, but you need to preserve appellate record. Weigh this against jury reaction.

    4. Admissible substantive evidence. Object if it will soften impact by explaining.

D. Admissibility for another purpose, for example, speed to show force of impact when liability admitted.

III. Manner and Method of Excluding Evidence

A. Make objections in laymen's terms. When reviewing rules of evidence, summarize rules in laymen's language.

B. Timing.

    1. If question is improper, object before answer.

    2. If question is proper and answer improper, move to strike after answer.

    3. Ignore unresponsive or incompetent answers unless answer will open door to prejudicial evidence.

C. General or specific objections.

    1. State specific grounds for appellate record. Overruling general objection is not an error unless evidence is inadmissible under any circumstance.

    2. Objection of immateriality and irrelevancy are specific.

    3. Objection to competency must be made with specific reason.

D. Motion to strike answer.

    1. If motion to strike answer is granted, move to have jury disregard answer.

    2. If failure to connect up testimony after objection, move to strike prior testimony.

    3. If witness refuses to submit to cross-exam, move to strike direct testimony.

    4. If witness fails to return to court for cross-exam, move to strike direct testimony. Move for mistrial if testimony is harmful and witness is unlikely to appear at second trial.

E. Presence of jury—in or out.

    1. Before trial, anticipate objections to substantive evidence.
       a. Pretrial conference.
       b. Motion in limine.

    2. At trial.
       a. Objection to form of question—in presence of jury.
          1) With leading question, phrase objection so jury realizes that lawyer is testifying rather than witness.
          2) Phrase objection to show you are not being dilatory.
          3) Phrase objection so jury becomes irritated with opposing lawyer for delays or unfair advantage.
       b. Objection to substantive evidence—exclude jury. Reference to evidence in argument may influence juror.
       c. Give sound reason for excluding jury so there is no implication of hiding evidence.

F. Obtain ruling on objections.

    1. Record for appeal.

    2. If provisional admission of evidence is never connected, move to strike.

IV. Proffer of Evidence

    A. Protecting record. Make a proffer of any evidence ruled inadmissible.

    B. Introduction of background and sociological evidence normally other wise inadmissible.

        1. To educate court.

        2. To support award on appeal.

        Appendix sample of witness order for simple auto collision case.

          1) Investigating officer.
          2) Defendant, if significant admissions can be gained.
          3) Eyewitness.
          4) Plaintiff.
          5) Other witnesses on liability issues.
          6) Medical records librarian.
          7) Doctors.
          8) Lay-medical witnesses.

Forms in Chapter 13

13 | Cross-Examination

I. Introduction

Cross-examination is the classic flashpoint and challenge of going to trial. It requires preparation and control. The goal of direct is for the witness to have a personal conversation with the jury, and tell his or her story. In cross-examination, everything changes. The lawyer is the focus, and the goal is for you to control the witness and make your points, not for the witness to retell his or her story. No advice is clearer than the late great Irving Younger's "Ten Commandments of Cross-Examination":[1]

1. Be brief.
2. Use short questions, plain words.
3. Always ask leading questions.
4. Do not ask a question unless you already know the answer.
5. Listen to the witness's answer.
6. Do not quarrel with the witness.
7. Do not allow the witness to repeat his direct testimony
8. Do not permit the witness to explain his answers.
9. Do not ask one too many questions.
10. Save the ultimate point of your cross for summation.

II. Three Types of Cross-Examination

There are essentially three different kinds of cross-examination: constructive, destructive, and credibility. The cross-examination of a particular witness may include one, two, or even all three of these types. Always begin with any constructive cross (Why attack a witness before he or she has helped you?), and then generally move to credibility, then destructive. The lines between them may sometimes blur, but it is worth considering each one separately here.

Constructive Cross

The common image of cross-examination as a pitched battle can lead to distortions of the process and lost opportunities. The realities of the trial process are that parties must often call and rely on witnesses who have things to say that can help both sides. The common phrase is that parties "take their witnesses as they find them." Thus, the first question you should ask in considering any cross examination is, "How can this witness help my case?" How can you use the witness constructively?

Constructive cross can be surprisingly effective because it is such a surprise to the trier of fact. Juries usually share the misperception of cross-examination as war. Therefore, any positive testimony from the other side's witness has the special luster of an admission by an opponent. Testimony that would be ordinary and unimpressive from your own witnesses on direct can have great impact if drawn from the other side's witnesses on cross.

Think creatively with each witness. Can you put a positive spin on what he or she has said on direct? Are there other issues or facts that you can raise through them? The possibilities are endless, but a few examples might help:

- A record keeper might be able to testify on cross about the existence or absence of certain other documents.
- An employee or colleague called to testify about one incident may have favorable information on others.
- An expert may have testified in another case on a similar issue, or even the same issue, in a way more favorable to your client.

Preparing for constructive cross requires as much, or sometimes more, thought and effort by you and your client as does any other kind. As always, preparation is the key.

Credibility

This includes attacking the witness's credibility directly on the subject matter of his or her testimony or on other issues. The rules of evidence and a judge's patience may sometimes limit impeachment on collateral issues. However, if it is an important witness and a well-prepared cross, courts often allow considerable latitude.

Effective credibility cross requires a high level of preparation and precision. Any time you have a witness's own words, you must be prepared to use them and back them up precisely. Vague questions followed by fishing through transcripts and files loses the impact and loses the jury. On the other hand, if you have the witness's own words, never accept anything less in cross-examination.

Other avenues for credibility cross include any prior criminal record, other prior dishonesty or bad acts, or other evidence tending to show dishonesty. Another approach is to show bias or motive for lying: involvement in the case, relationship with the parties, and so on. In general, a jury is much more likely to believe that a witness is lying if it is clear that the witness has lied in the past or if you present a good reason *why* the witness is lying.

Destructive

This involves a direct assault on the witness's testimony. It can come from general directions, including attacks on:

- bias;
- memory;
- ability to observe;
- problems with story.

III. Planning Cross-Examination

Planning and Preparation

These are the keys to effective cross-examination. Start early. As soon as you become aware of a potential witness for the other side, set up a cross-examination file for that witness. On an ongoing basis, direct notes, copies of documents, and any other relevant material to that file. Think about how you should approach the cross-examination. What is the theme for that witness?

In preparing to cross-examine any witness, you should use your own witnesses and your client as sources of information. Show experts' reports and resumes to your expert. Show the depositions to your client or appropriate witnesses. Ask them where the witness is in error and, if the witness is the expert, ask your expert what you should do on cross-examination.

Attached are Forms 13–1 to 13–4, a series of checklists that may be helpful in your preparation:

Form 13–1. Checklist for Preparing Cross-Examination
Form 13–2. Checklist of General Purposes and Techniques for Cross-Examination

These are *not* witness outlines; you will never ask one witness about all these areas. Rather, they are intended to help the ongoing process of brainstorming and analyzing in preparation for cross.

The Decision to Cross

At every step of preparing for cross, you should stop and consider whether any is necessary. You must evaluate the witness, his or her direct testimony, and your case in making your decision. As lawyers, our first reaction (and often our client's) is that we must conduct a vigorous cross-examination. To counter this, the decision not to conduct any cross requires a careful analysis of the potential damage a cross-examination may cause.

In making a decision regarding cross-examination, you should put yourself in the jury's place and consider the following:

A. Has the witness hurt your case? If not, and there is nothing constructive, do not cross-examine.
B. Is the witness's testimony on a peripheral or important issue?
  1. Danger of emphasizing peripheral issues.
  2. Danger of expanding or repeating direct testimony.
C. Can you realistically get the witness to give any testimony favorable to your case?
  1. Unsuccessful cross reemphasizes points.
  2. Successful cross can move attention from harmful direct to admissions or other issues.
D. Was the witness credible?
E. Do you know how the witness will answer your questions?
F. Can the witness be impeached or discredited?
G. How can cross-examination help or hurt your closing argument?
H. Consider the alternative ways to rebut harmful direct.
  1. Other witnesses—either on cross or rebuttal.
  2. Documentary evidence.

Sometimes the most effective cross is two words: "No questions." If you are in doubt as to whether you should conduct a cross-examination, *do not*. If the direct testimony is merely a formality on introductory matters or on facts not in issue, waive cross-examination. If the witness is invulnerable to cross, waive it. Impress the jury. Dismiss the witness with those two words and move on.

Witness Notebook

The image of Perry Mason getting up to destroy a witness on cross with just a few notes from direct examination scribbled on a pad is not one you should emulate. In today's litigation, lawyers usually have a pretty good idea of who the other side's witnesses will be and what they will say before they take the stand. Thus, it becomes possible—and essential—to prepare witness outlines and notebooks for cross-examination just like those described above for direct. There are two principal differences:

- Greater precision and backup.
- Adapting to direct.

1. <u>Greater precision and backup.</u> If control is the key to cross, precision is the key to control. Your witness outline and notebook is what gives you this precision. For example, if the witness has said something that has been written down, whether in a document, statement, deposition or whatever, your notebook should:

    a. Quote it exactly in your outline.
    b. Provide the exact cite, (page, line, and so forth).
    c. Include a highlighted working copy for you.
    d. Include or reference a copy for the witness.

    In this way, the precise words and, if necessary, the precise backup, are all at your fingertips, and the witness cannot use vagueness or uncertainty to blur his or her prior words.

    Precision in preparation helps you with the "Three Cs" of command of the courtroom: Confidence, Control and Credibility. These in turn create their own advantage: once witnesses realize how well prepared you are, they will often concede more and fight less, out of fear that you will just nail them again.

2. <u>Adapting to direct</u>

    The better prepared you are, the better you can listen and react to the direct. A good witness outline is generously spaced with only one topic per page. This should leave plenty of room to plug in statements or ideas from direct examination. That leaves only the question of when and how to do this. If you know that you will have time (lunch break, overnight) you can wait to write your ideas. Otherwise, you have to find the time during lulls in the direct or other breaks. Always draw a line down the page of your notes and leave space on your right for notes for cross (see, Form 13–5). If you are likely to be really pressed for time, try this: as you make notes during direct in the right hand column of questions or follow-up for cross, number those notes; then you can just insert the numbers in your witness outline and can easily refer to your notes as you go.

IV. Effective Cross-Examination

Leading Questions

Nowhere is the contrast between direct and cross as clear as in the use of leading questions. In cross-examination, *every* question should be leading. Right from the start (do not wait until you get into trouble) train the witness and the jury that you will ask the questions and the witness's job is to say "yes" or "no." However, to exercise this kind of control takes careful preparation and patience. Just leading is not enough; your questions must also be short and absolutely clear. The longer the question, the easier it is for the witness to waffle or evade. Be patient. Take your time. The wall you are building to enclose the witness must be assembled one brick at a time or it will not hold.

The most common mistake lawyers make on cross is to try to do too much in one question. In direct examination, we said that a red flag should go up if a question is longer than three to four words. Surprisingly, the rule is not much different on cross. Questions on cross should be short, clear statements by you with a question mark at the end. If your statement is more than four or five words long, stop. Why are you asking it that way? Break the question down into its component parts and build slowly, inexorably toward your conclusion. That way you will keep control of the witness and increase the chances that the jury will follow along and come to the right conclusion.

Turning your short statement of fact into a short question is relatively simple. The easiest way is to just precede it or follow it with a question phrase. For example, suppose an eyewitness's ability to see is relevant, and your evidence is that it was foggy the day in question. On cross, don't ask the open question ("What was the weather that day?") or even the simple leading question ("Was it foggy that day?"). Take command with a simple statement ("It was foggy that day") turned into a question, for example:

Prefix: "Isn't it true that it was foggy that day?"

Suffix: "It was foggy that day, wasn't it?"

You can vary your question phrases, but don't vary the basic structure (see, Form 13–5, Sample Question Phrases).

If you follow this structure consistently, you will often have the witness so conditioned to the statement-as-a-question, that you can sometimes take away the question phrase, and just make the statement and have the witness respond:

Q: It was cloudy that day.
A: Yes.
Q: And drizzling too.
A: Yes.

In this way, you can command and control the witness just by the way you structure your questions.

Juries like to discover things for themselves, rather than be lectured. Short questions allow them to come to the conclusion you want them to reach, and the impact will be much greater when they discover it themselves. A series of facts is not an obstacle to be overcome with a conclusory question, but an opportunity to confront the witness with a litany of short, similar punchy questions that build toward your conclusion. For example, if time is an issue:

Conclusory	Litany
You had lots of time to act before Smith appeared, didn't you?	You had time to do X You had time to do Y You had time to do Z

If your questions are short and clear, then never accept an answer other than "yes" or "no." If your questions are long and convoluted, neither the judge nor the jury will sympathize with your desire to get a yes or no answer. However, if your questions are simple and crystal clear, it is the witness who will lose favor if he or she resists. Sometimes the most effective cross-examination is just repeating, (or have the court reporter repeat) a simple question over and over until it is clear that the witness is being evasive.

Use of Documents/Statements

First, find out what notes or documents the witness has used or been shown before (or during) testimony and get them. Some witnesses will almost always have reviewed their notes or files before testifying. Examples are police, doctors, investigators, and expert witnesses. You may consider asking the court to let you question the witnesses to lay a foundation for an objection. If allowed, you can ask the witnesses what they used to refresh their memory and, if they acknowledge they used some type of notes, you should ask to see them and then object to the testimony if they refuse. These notes may contain information adverse to the other side or material that will aid you in your cross-examination.

Next, make sure you have any prior statements by the witness that might be relevant to the subject. Remember, statements come in many forms from the informal (notes, memos, e-mail, and so forth) to the formal (letters, tapes, reports, and affidavits) to the legalistic (depositions, interrogatories, testimony in other cases). There may be gems out there that you do not know about if you do not pursue all possible options.

Finally, be comfortable with documents in the courtroom. Part of being organized is having what you need available. If you want something read, *you* read it, and have the witness confirm that *you* read it accurately.

Once you have something in a document or a statement, never let go. Do not accept less than the witness's statement that is most favorable to you and make it clear to the jury if the witness is playing games. I refer to CLAP, the process for dealing with a witness who has changed his or her story:

- <u>C</u>onfirm
- <u>L</u>ock In
- <u>A</u>ccredit
- <u>P</u>ursue

1. <u>Confirm</u> the witness's current story. Try to cut out any room for maneuvering.
2. <u>Lock</u> In the witness as clearly as possible to his or her version of the story and the importance of the testimony, without raising too much suspicion.
3. <u>Accredit the prior statement.</u> Whether it is sworn testimony or contemporaneous notes, you want to make clear its importance and credibility. Although I put this as third in this sequence, with good planning you may want to do this as an early foundational matter, *before* you start this process and before the witness begins to think that he or she might want to change it. Then you can come back to that earlier testimony ("Remember at the beginning of your cross, you testified about how important it was to be truthful in your file memos. . . ."), and restate it here.

4. Pursue the inconsistency, depending on which version you like better. Make the conflict clear to the jury. Accept nothing less than agreement with the version you prefer or acknowledgment of the conflict or change.

Demonstrative Evidence

Many lawyers who would not hesitate to use or create demonstrative evidence for direct do not think about it for cross. Yet the need and the opportunity are still great. You are still trying to teach the jury, while emphasizing key points. Consider a wide range of graphics or other exhibits such as:

- blowups of key documents;
- drawings or maps to highlight points;
- time lines or other "chalks;" and
- scale models.

Expert Witnesses

The opponent's expert sometimes presents the greatest challenge in cross-examination. If you do not conduct a cross-examination, the jury may be left with the impression that the expert is correct and that his or her opinion should not be questioned. If you do cross-examine, you are facing a witness who generally knows far more than you do about the subject and has had experience testifying.

Effective cross-examination of an expert requires advance preparation. Pretrial discovery of expert's reports and opinions is essential. Make a list of points you will cover. Use direct examination to add additional points or to note testimony that will assist you on the points you have prepared.

If the expert is not qualified to testify, you should ask the court to allow you to question the witness for the purpose of laying a foundation for an objection. Your questions should be leading and should go directly to the basis of your proposed objection. One should use this approach with caution, since an objection that is overruled will look like a defeat and may enhance the credibility of the witness. If upon completing your questioning, you do not believe an objection will be sustained, just state that you have no objections. The jury will see you as fair-minded and not an obstructionist.

In all but the most unusual and dramatic situation, do not challenge the expert head-on. The jury will generally assume the expert knows his or her field of expertise. Your credibility may be seriously damaged if you lose the confrontation. Pick out the issues, foundations, facts or opinions that you know you can challenge effectively and leave the rest alone.

KISS

Just as cross-examination highlights the drama of trial advocacy, it also highlights one of its most important lessons: "Keep It Simple, Stupid," (KISS). The more time you spend preparing your cross-examination, the more ideas you will have. As a result, one of the most common mistakes in cross is to do too much, to ask too many questions about too many issues. When everything is important, nothing is important. Your best point may become lost in what seems to the jury as nit-picking. The challenge is to examine all the ideas and avenues you have come up with in preparation and put most of them aside. Focus on the handful of points that are truly clear and effective. Make your points and sit down.

V. Style of Examination

You should always rely on your own style. If you try to copy someone else, you will not appear natural, and you will lose credibility with the jury. Generally remain calm and courteous. Always appear under control.

A hostile, aggressive approach may be effective at the beginning of cross-examination to overwhelm the witness. However, there is a real danger of generating jury sympathy for the witness. Generally use this approach in climax when disclosing significant contradictions or bias. It may also be effective, if used carefully, with the confused witness, hostile witness, and experts.

An ingratiating manner or appearance of ineptness may be adopted with the cocky, know-it-all witness to encourage brash, implausible statements. This approach should be used only when you are reasonably sure it will work.

Above all, be yourself. Respond appropriately to the witness, but in a way that keeps you as the focus of attention and preserves your credibility.

Endnote

1. IRVING YOUNGER, THE ART OF CROSS-EXAMINATION, 21–31 (Section of Litigation Monograph Series No. 1, 1976).

Further Reading

Bailey, F. Lee. *Cross-Examination in Criminal Trials*. Rochester, NY: Lawyers Co-operative Publishing Co., 1978.

Belli, Melvin M. *Modern Trials*. Vol. 4. St. Paul, Minn.: West Publishing Co., 1982.

Busch, Francis Xavier. *Law and Tactics in Jury Trials*. Vol. 3. New York: Bobbs-Merrill Co., Inc., 1960.

Iannuzzi, John Nicholas. *Cross-Examination: The Mosaic Art*. Englewood Cliffs, NJ: Prentice-Hall, 1982.

Mauet, Thomas A. *Fundamentals of Trial Techniques*. Boston: Little, Brown and Company, 1980.

Redfield, Roy Addis. *Cross-Examination and the Witness*. Mundelein, Ill.: Callaghan, 1963.

Wellman, Francis Lewis. *The Art of Cross-Examination*. Garden City, NY: Garden City Publishing Co., 1948.

Younger, Irving. *The Art of Cross-Examination*. Chicago: American Bar Association, Section of Litigation, Monograph Series No. 1, 1976.

13-1 CHECKLIST FOR PREPARING CROSS-EXAMINATION

A. Background.
  _____ Name.
  _____ Address.
  _____ Marital status.
  _____ Children.
  _____ Occupation.

B. Relationship to client or opponent.
  _____ Knowledge of client prior to incident.
  _____ Knowledge of opponent prior to incident.
  _____ Relationship to client or opponent.

C. Knowledge of incident.
  _____ How witness knows of incident.
  _____ Prior statements (written).
  _____ Prior statements or discussions (oral).
  _____ Financial interest in outcome.
  _____ Bias toward client.
  _____ Payment for testimony.
  _____ Ability to observe and recall.
  _____ Witness's conduct in relation to incident.

D. Preparation for testifying.
  _____ Who asked him to testify?
  _____ Was he subpoenaed?
  _____ Did he discuss case with anyone?
  _____ Did he discuss testimony with lawyer?
  _____ Did he attend meetings with other witnesses?
  _____ Did he read materials prior to testimony?
  _____ Did he prepare notes after incident or prior to testimony?
  _____ Did he read prior statements or depositions?
  _____ Does he have a personal interest in outcome?
  _____ Will he receive any payment for testimony?
  _____ Has he testified in other cases?

E. Expert witnesses.

_____ Qualifications.

_____ Relevant experience.

_____ Materials used in forming opinion.

_____ Opinion.

_____ Explanation of opinion and reasons.

_____ Prior publications.

_____ Obtain transcripts of Prior Testimony.

_____ Has he read literature from other experts in the area?

_____ Have your expert review other experts' reports.

_____ Professional fees charged?

_____ Frequency of testimony?

_____ Is subject matter outside area of education?

_____ Would opinion change if facts change?

_____ Obtain agreement with your expert.

_____ Force expert to use common language.

_____ Show witness has no first-hand knowledge.

_____ Show witness testifies for lawyer at other times.

_____ Show source of information (for example, opponent) may be unreliable.

_____ Determine if expert has reviewed all records or just part.

_____ Show expert has not dealt with or treated your client.

F. Credibility or impeachment.

_____ Motive.

_____ Bias.

_____ Prejudice.

_____ Prior inconsistent statements.

_____ Prior testimony.

_____ Memory of details.

_____ Pleadings.

_____ Omissions from records, reports, or prior statements.

_____ Criminal convictions.

_____ Learned treatises, periodicals, or pamphlets.

13-2 CHECKLIST OF GENERAL PURPOSES AND TECHNIQUES FOR CROSS-EXAMINATION

A. General purpose is to develop evidence in support of preplanned summation attacking credibility of adverse witnesses.

1. Discredit witness's testimony—contradictions, modifications, retractions, errors, confusion in story.

2. Discredit witness's credibility—conduct, interest, bias, reputation, qualifications.

3. Obtain helpful testimony.
    a. Discredit other witness's testimony.
    b. Corroborate other witness's favorable testimony.
    c. Obtain direct favorable testimony.

4. Lay foundation for impeachment—by other witness or writings.

5. Lay foundation for objection—incompetent testimony.

B. Application of general purposes.

1. Discredit witness's testimony.
    a. Prior inconsistent statement—written or oral.
        1) When to use.
            a) If entire statement admissible, use only if overall effect favorable to your case.
            b) Limit offer of statement for impeachment purposes only— limits to impeaching sections (see local rules).
        2) Dishonest witness.
            a) Commit witness unequivocally to testimony by recovering direct before laying foundation.
            b) Pin witness down to all details before contradicting testimony.
        3) Honest, forgetful witness.
            a) Use statement to prod memory and correct testimony.
            b) Foundation—Identify statement, time, and place.
                (1) Confront witness with written statement; describe oral statement.
                (2) If denied, introduce document into evidence or produce witnesses to verify.
            c) Adverse party—no foundation required. May be introduced on your direct as admission. Strategy—Better to lay foundation and confront on cross; witness has no time to think of explanation and fairness before jury.

    d) Establish circumstances of statement if tend to reinforce impeachment (such as solemnity of deposition) after statement introduced.

  b. Contradiction by public documents or private records. Foundation—identification and admission of records.

  c. Improbability of story—inherent illogic.

    1) Get witness to admit each link in logical chain of facts.

    2) Point out illogic in direct, and obtain retraction or modification.

    3) If impossibility of story to be proved by other witnesses or documentary evidence on in direct or in rebuttal, pin witness down to all details to foreclose subsequent explanation.

  d. Improbability of story—faulty observation or recollection. Factors to develop:

    1) Personality of witness, his occupation, and so on, as bearing on his mental acuteness or retentiveness.

    2) Suddenness of events narrated and time in which happened.

    3) Minuteness of time in which any detail occurred.

    4) Number of things happening at time of accident that could confuse perception and observation.

    5) Number of details of the sudden crisis remembered by witness.

    6) Time when witness first tried to synthesize all impressions into whole.

    7) Lack of personal knowledge—amount of discussion with other witness and possible transference of ideas.

    8) Manner in which details by witness check against details by other witness in better position to observe.

    9) Distinguish recollection from judgment, assumptions, or conjecture.

  e. Conduct inconsistent with validity or belief in claim. Establish all instances of such conduct.

  f. Error in facts or basis for assumptions (similar to illogical story).

    1) Commit witness to facts by reiterating.

    2) Point out error or lack of essential facts, and obtain retraction or modification—or establish impossibility.

    3) If have strong expert, use him to point out error and contradiction.

  g. Inconsistencies with other witness's testimony.

    1) Honest error—develop and correct on cross.

    2) Dishonest—attack with other independent evidence or witness.

2. Discredit witness.

  a. Qualifications to render opinion.

    1) Obviously unqualified—attack in voir dire or when submitted on direct.

       2) Questionable qualifications—attack on cross.

  b. Defects in validity of opinion due to impairment of physical or mental powers of observation or recollection.

  c. Conviction of crime.

       1) Federal Rule—crimes of dishonesty, false statement (perjury, fraud, embezzlement, and so on), or felony admissible in court's discretion.

           a) Ten-year time limit or advance notice to adversary.

           b) Evidence allowed—name of crime, time, place of punishment.

           c) No extrinsic evidence such as court records.

  d. Noncriminal acts of misconduct tending to show witness is not believable. Federal rule—court's discretion and only if probative of veracity or character of witness.

  e. Reputation for truth in community. Federal rule—allows witness opinion as to another's reputation based on personal knowledge.

  f. Interest, bias, prejudice.

       1) Pecuniary interest in outcome.

       2) Relationship to party—friend, business, employer.

       3) Hostile, biased, or prejudicial statements or acts.

           a) Lay foundation for proof by other witnesses.

           b) Question in detail to develop absurd or untenable position.

           c) Several witnesses—show that testimony is alike in minute detail and that they conferred with each other.

  g. Questionable or unworthy conduct in relation to parties or event.

  h. Lies on collateral matters.

       1) Use where unexplainable and apparently done out of bias or interest.

       2) Use where done in more than one instance.

3. Obtain helpful testimony.

  a. Use nonhostile witness.

  b. Amplify and reinforce favorable direct. Useful when opponent's theory erroneous or rebuttable.

  c. Elicit admissions.

  d. Lay foundation for your direct evidence that will be based on facts presented by adverse witnesses.

4. Lay foundation for impeachment.

  a. Prior inconsistent statements (see above).

  b. Reputation, bias, criminal conduct (see above).

5. Lay foundation for objection. Interruption of direct to conduct cross-examination specifically to lay foundation.

    a.   Interrupt direct regarding agreement to show agreement in writing and support objection of best-evidence rule.

    b.   Interrupt direct regarding statements to show privilege.

C. Method of examination.

  1. Keep it short and distinct. Make only one or two points on witness's credibility.

  2. Use leading questions—yes or no answers.

  3. Avoid broad, open-ended questions—how and why. Exception—exploratory examination with disinterested or obviously untruthful witness who damaged case. Amplify it to discover weaknesses.

    a.   Develop inconsistencies or contradictions in details.

    b.   Develop expressions of conjecture—"I think," "I believe," "Probably."

    c.   Develop statements without foundation or apparent reason.

  4. Dealing with evasive witness. If the witness is evasive, become firm in your questioning. Insist that the question be answered and, if necessary, ask the court to instruct the witness to answer. If the witness tries to outsmart you, he or she will lose the sympathy of the jury, thereby assisting you in using a firmer approach.

    a.   Don't allow witness to explain every question; may explain on redirect.

    b.   Don't allow witness to reword question and answer that.

    c.   Don't allow witness to answer question with question.

    d.   Judge aid—Move to strike as unresponsive, and ask judge to instruct witness.

    e.   Don't ask judge to instruct witness, but repeat question exactly over and over after asking witness to answer yes or no and explain in redirect.

    f.   Get witness to acknowledge conditions or explanations unjustified.

    g.   Cross-examine just enough to show jury that he is evasive.

  5. Concentrate on predetermined weak point in opponent's case.

  6. Obtaining and keeping admissions.

    a.   Avoid "Isn't it a fact" questions.

    b.   Upon hesitation to make simple admissions, ask "There isn't any doubt about that, is there?"

    c.   If hesitation coupled with answers to previous questions indicates admission, pass on.

    d.   Upon obtaining admission, move on.

13-3 CHECKLIST FOR CROSS-EXAMINATION OF EXPERTS—GENERAL

A.   General purposes and rules as above.

B.   Attack qualifications.

   1.   Object on direct when submitted as expert unless certain can discredit witness qualifications on cross.

   2.   Get to admit that not specialist or subspecialist in specific field in case.

   3.   Get to admit his area of practice does not include issues in case.

   4.   Get to admit your expert is specialist or active practitioner in field.

C.   Use of hypothetical questions on cross-examination.

   1.   Agreement or evasion with selected hypotheses most favorable to your case. Effective with strong supporting evidence for hypotheses.

   2.   When hypotheses on direct are not fully supported by evidence for purpose of testing witness knowledge or opinions.

   3.   Hypothetical question regarding possibilities. Where expert says accident probably not cause of injury, cross-exam questions may ask if possible for this type of accident to cause this type of injury.

D.   Attack expert with texts, authorities, and so on.

   1.   Witness acknowledges he consulted text in forming opinion.

   2.   Witness acknowledges text is authoritative.
        a.   Experts in field rely on book.
        b.   Book regarded as authoritative.
        c.   Book is standard work among experts in field.

   3.   Get witness to accept credentials of various authors, their publishers, and institutions while refusing to concede authoritative nature of tests.
        a.   Get articles by institutions known to public.
        b.   Get articles written by doctors at local medical schools.
        c.   Discover in depositions or in library the works experts consider authoritative.
        d.   Establish witness familiarity with publication.
        e.   Read statement; don't paraphrase.

4. Federal rules allow learned treatise as evidence. Use own witness to establish authority.

5. Check authenticity of articles and references, and Shepardize.

E. Attack expert on standards.

1. Get witness to take position that act or product met standards or that no standards existed.

2. Introduce and read standards to jury.

F. Show incorrect basis or reason for opinion.

1. Determine factual basis for conclusions where different from your expert.

2. Show witness has no personal knowledge and got all facts from party. Can attack expert's credibility by attacking party's credibility.

3. Show that one or more main supporting factors are nonexistent or improper—in basis for opinion or hypothetical on direct. Ask if additional facts might affect his opinion.

4. Show witness did not consider other factors favoring your view.

5. Show failure to conduct certain tests.

6. Show testimony contradicts his own research or file notes.

G. Show that opinion based wholly or in part on subjective judgment.

1. Where conclusion based on overall picture, question witness on isolated, separate components.

2. Ask witness if he could be wrong. If yes, use. If no, ask if ever been wrong.
   a. Ask if he has ever been a consultant with other experts where there was split opinion and he was right.
   b. If so, ask if the opposite is true. Any answer can be used.

13-4 CHECKLIST FOR CROSS-EXAMINATION OF MEDICAL EXPERT

A. Financial bias.

   1. Determine before trial how frequently doctor testifies and examines for or is retained by plaintiffs or defendants.
       a. Number of times per week used by plaintiff or defendant firms or insurance companies.
       b. Charge per exam, per report, per pretrial conference, and per court appearance.
       c. Number of times in prior year doctor made exams of plaintiff's or defendant's clients and number of times testified in court. Establish by starting with exams per day and multiply.

   2. Determine before trial number of items in same time period doctor did same—exams and testimony—for opposite side.

   3. Obtain transcripts of prior paid testimony and review for inconsistencies.

B. Qualifications.

   1. Explore in deposition.
       a. Board certified.
       b. Outside specialty.

   2. Source of information—*Directory of Medical Specialists*.

C. Attack of medical opinions.

   1. Use discovery to determine what doctor will say.

   2. Weigh and evaluate doctor's opinion.
       a. Review and discuss with your doctor.
       b. Determine where vulnerable.
       c. Consider what is not in reports as well as what's in them.

   3. Read all books, articles, etc., by doctor.
       a. See *Index Medicus*.
       b. Use authorities, texts, and so forth, to impeach.

   4. Review all notes and records used by doctor on direct.
       a. Obtain access by objections on direct.
       b. Get doctor to admit has no independent recollection of exam—sees so many patients over years.

    c. Once admits using notes and has no independent recollection, then tired to notes and report.

    d. failed to conduct classic tests (if missing from notes), then difficult to say he did them.

    e. Use reports and notes to limit evasiveness.

5. Using medical texts.
    a. On deposition determine what books, other sources, expert considers authoritative.
    b. Determine names of teachers studied under.
    c. Determine leading doctors in field.
    d. Determine basic medical texts on question or in his library.
    e. Determine any publications he may have authored.
    f. Get dolor to accept credentials of various authors, their publishers, and institutions while refusing to concede authorities.
    g. Check local rule on admissibility.

6. Length of exam and treatment of client.
    a. Doctor not treating physician.
    b. Doctor saw plaintiff only once for short time.
       1) Saw many other patients same morning or afternoon.
       2) Entire exam took ___ minutes, including time in obtaining history.
       3) Examined party only; did not treat.

D. Examples of cross-examination to obtain concessions and use.

1. Establish plaintiff was cooperative and honest in claims.
    a. Foundation—by experience doctor can tell a malingerer.
    b. Responses to tests were consistent with claims.
    c. Plaintiff was not a malingerer.

2. Establish function of injured joint or area. Lay foundation for testimony on complications after injury.

3. Admissions.
    a. Not treating doctor; examined plaintiff once—only for purpose of report to defendant's insurance company and for testimony.
    b. Does not know plaintiff as well as treating doctor, and plaintiff's doctor in better position to give complete picture of extent and nature of injury.
    c. Treatment by plaintiff's doctor was proper for type of injury diagnosed.

    d.   Get expert to concede plaintiff doctor's qualifications.

    e.   Difference of opinion between doctors not unusual, and cannot say with certainty that plaintiff doctor wrong.

4.   Subjective complaints.

    a.   Doctor cannot say plaintiff does not feel pain—only cannot find objective signs.

    b.   Concede that he treats his own patients on basis of subjective complaints without objective signs.

    c.   Tenderness is significant sign of nonvisible injury or underlying condition or pathology.

    d.   Review complaints of pain in history and exam by plaintiff's doctor.

    e.   Review complaints of pain at time of defendant exam—consistent.

    f.   Plaintiff's subjective complaints of pain in certain areas of body consistent with plaintiff's evidence.

    g.   If assume truth and accuracy of complaints, must agree with plaintiff's expert's diagnosis.

5.   Recovery marked by periods of remission and exacerbation; no way of knowing if on his exam plaintiff had a good or bad day.

6.   Doctor did not determine if plaintiff had taken drugs or muscle relaxants prior to exam. This could affect plaintiff's responses or mask symptoms.

7.   Negative X-rays. Does not preclude soft-tissue injury and other conditions. Supporting muscles, tissues, ligaments, not shown on X-ray.

8.   Attack method of exam if faulty or not complete.

    a.   One exam not as good as series of exams.

    b.   After one exam, doctor will form tentative diagnosis and occasionally later decides it's wrong.

9.   Causation.

    a.   Admit doctor has no idea of severity of trauma.

    b.   Admit no knowledge of damage to car, speed, and so forth.

    c.   Accident is only cause shown for whatever symptoms of injury contained in defendant's doctor's history and findings.

10. Disability—prognosis.

    a.   Concede doctor has little knowledge of plaintiff's specific work duties or leisure activities.

    b.   Disability opinion based on this insufficient knowledge.

    c.   Admit acute condition may become chronic.

11. Defense of preexisting arthritis of spine.
    a. Admit arthritis present in most over forty years old and frequently causes no pain or disability.
    b. However, makes affected person more prone to injury and delays healing process.

12. Reemphasize plaintiff's case by sticking to accepted medical propositions of plaintiff's injury—muscle spasm characteristics and meaning.

13-5 SAMPLE QUESTION PHRASES

<u>Cross-Examination:</u> Put desired answer into statement form the precede or follow it with a question phrase

<u>Sample Question Phrases:</u>

Follow:
    Isn't it a fact that
    Isn't it true that
    It's fair to say, isn't it, that   **+ Statement**
    It's true, isn't it, Witness, that
    It's a fact, isn't it, that

Precede:

    didn't you
    weren't you
    haven't you
    hadn't you
    did you
    were you
    have you
    did you not
    were you not
    have you not

Statement +

    isn't that right
    isn't that a fact

    that's so, isn't it
    true
    that's true
    correct
    that's correct
    that's correct, isn't it
    right
    isn't that right
    isn't that fair
    that's fair, isn't it
    isn't that fair to say

    is there
    was there
    were there

    was it not
    wasn't it

Forms in Chapter 14

14 | Rebuttal and Post-Trial Motions

Rebuttal is the rebuilding of the plaintiff's case-in-chief and the dismantling of the opponent's case. The general rule is to put on your strongest evidence in the case-in-chief and not to rely on rebuttal as a substitute for the case-in-chief. Rebuttal evidence is (1) to explain away, qualify, or directly contradict the defense case; and (2) to support and rehabilitate the case-in-chief.

Do you have a witness (or witnesses) who can contradict the evidence presented in the defense case? Can they discredit the credibility of the defense witnesses? Does the evidence attack a critical point of the defense? Does the evidence support a significant part of the case-in-chief?

By centering the attack on the central issues of the case, you can lead jurors to the conclusion that the smaller matters may be unimportant. Do not spend time on extraneous details. The selection of strong evidence and strong witnesses for rebuttal can leave the jury with an impression of the strength of your case.

The use of rebuttal witnesses can serve as an effective alternative or supplement to cross-examination. When the defendant has presented a witness who is very impressive and whose testimony is difficult to assault by a cross-examination, you should consider whether that testimony is subject to attack by a rebuttal witness. If so, to forgo cross-examination and attack by the rebuttal witness may lessen the first witness's opportunity to increase the damage. This is particularly true with expert witnesses where your own expert can explain, qualify, or contradict the testimony.

Rebuttal evidence is only admissible as a reply to new points introduced by your adversary. Any competent evidence that explains, repels, disproves, or otherwise contradicts your adversary's proof is admissible. Normally you cannot utilize rebuttal to attack matters that you developed on cross-examination, as opposed to those developed by your adversary. You cannot use it to introduce testimony that is not in rebuttal of your adversary's proof and does not tend to dispute it. You do not have the right to simply introduce evidence that should have been presented in your case-in-chief.

You can, however, use any witnesses in rebuttal, whether or not they testified in the case-in-chief. It may be necessary, in the case of rebutting expert-witness testimony elicited by your opponent, to present a number of experts whose testimony contradicts the opponent's proof.

Sometimes it is important to deny statements made about your client or your client's actions in rebuttal. (The jury may expect that such a statement would draw righteous indignation and denial.)

Planning is the key to an effective rebuttal. In almost every jurisdiction, the rules now require a disclosure by each side of the intended witnesses and the subject matter of their testimony. Careful study and analysis of the possible witnesses will help you to plan your rebuttal attack. Your opponent will have committed himself to a theory of the case that you can then assault with your rebuttal witnesses. Where necessary, be sure to lay appropriate foundation for rebuttal testimony in your case-in-chief, or during cross-examination of your adversary's witnesses.

Hold pure rebuttal evidence until end of case. This will allow the defendant to commit to a point or theory. Lay foundations, if necessary, during cross-examination. However, be careful. Do not hold back good affirmative witnesses or evidence for rebuttal and thereby risk losing proof in your direct case if the direction of the defendant's case does not provide the opportunity for rebuttal.

Anticipate rebuttal, using limited rebuttal evidence during cross-examination. Introduce rebuttal evidence early if necessary to preserve prima facie case or if the witness will not be available for the rebuttal stage. Use it in your direct case to soften effect of anticipated strong adverse evidence in opponent's case.

Avoid pitfalls in rebuttal. Do not try too hard or try to do too much. Do not give the defendant the opportunity to cross-examine weak witnesses, or to rehash defense issues. Do not get bogged down in collateral issues; limit to one or two main points. Don't address weak points in your case unless you can either substantially and effectively destroy defendant's position or rehabilitate your own.

I. Post-Trial Motions

There are two categories of post-trial motions. The first category might be referred to as "housekeeping," as the motions are primarily for correcting or perfecting the record. The second category includes motions that go to the merits and can sometimes be dispositive of the case. Form 14–1 is a general checklist of motions. Form 14–2 contains a rough timetable. Always check your local rules.

In preparing for any post-trial motions, you must conduct a review of the evidence and proceedings at trial. You generally have an initial opportunity to review the trial proceedings while preparing final arguments. At this time, be alert for any indications that motions should be made to correct or perfect the record.

Has your opponent presented proof that was not legally admissible but was permitted on a promise to "connect it up"? If the connecting up did not occur, make a motion to strike the inadmissible portion of the record. If the case has not gone to the jury, you may also wish to request a curative instruction. However, you must weigh the value of striking the evidence from the record against the possible detrimental effect of bringing it to the jury's attention again.

Likewise if evidence admitted at trial is incompetent, as shown by the record, a motion to strike the incompetent matter from the record is in order. If there is a judgment entered and an error appears in it as a result of clerical oversight or omission, it is possible for you to move the court to correct such a clerical flaw.

Another consideration is whether issues were litigated that are outside the scope of the pleadings. If so, a motion to amend the pleadings to conform to the proof would be in order. In many jurisdictions this motion can be made at any time, even after the entry of judgment.

Your purpose in making the above motions is twofold: first, to allow the trial court to correct errors in the proceedings, and second, to perfect a clear record for appeal.

The second type of motion is issue dispositive. It includes a motion for a directed verdict at the conclusion of the evidence, a motion for judgment notwithstanding the verdict, or (in the event of a court trial) a motion for amended findings.

A motion for a directed verdict is commonly made at the conclusion of the plaintiff's case. It must be renewed after the close of all the evidence. Renewal of the motion for directed verdict is a prerequisite to a motion for judgment notwithstanding the verdict in most jurisdictions. (This motion is also sometimes referred to as a motion for an instructed verdict, for no suit, or for peremptory instruction.) It is basically a request for the court to rule that the evidence as presented is not sufficient to raise a question of fact upon which a jury could find for the opposing party.

A prerequisite to making the motion for directed verdict is genuine deficiencies in the proof of the opposition's case. Like the other motions, this is not something that should be done automatically; it should only be used when there is a genuine basis for the motion.

There is no requirement in the Federal Rules of Civil Procedure that a Rule 50 motion for directed verdict be in writing. Nevertheless, it is good practice to submit such a motion in writing in order to ensure that you have complied with the requirement for specificity of grounds as required by the rule. While you may not have a gift of prophecy to know exactly what grounds will arise in trial, with careful preparation certain grounds could be predicted with some accuracy, and such grounds can be stated on separate sheets to be attached to a written motion as they become applicable. Pick out three or four areas where your opponent's case is defective and set out in detail the specific grounds in which the proof is lacking. Remember that under the federal rules, a failure to state grounds for the motion with sufficient specificity may be grounds for denying the motion.

Before you move for a directed verdict at the close of the plaintiff's case, you should consider the potential danger of alerting opposing counsel to its weakness(es), thus inviting your opponent to correct the flaw by effective cross-examination or by reopening the case.

A motion for a judgment notwithstanding the verdict is used to test the legal sufficiency of the evidence. In this respect it is like a motion for directed verdict. The applicable test for granting the motion is the same as for a directed verdict. That is to say, the evidence presented leads to only one reasonable conclusion of the proper judgment.

In the federal rules, and in many state rules, a necessary prerequisite to a motion for judgment notwithstanding the verdict is the making of a motion for a directed verdict at the conclusion of all the evidence. Having made a motion for directed verdict earlier in the trial will not be sufficient. (However, this is not true in all jurisdictions. See, Minnesota Rules of Civil Procedure 50.02(1).)

While there is no specifically prescribed formula for such a motion, the safe procedure is to use the rule's own terms, move that the verdict and judgment entered be set aside, and have judgment in accordance with the earlier motion for a directed verdict. The motion must be brought within the time limits set out in the rules (Federal Rule of Civil Procedure 50(b)), as such time limits are mandatory. The motion for judgment notwithstanding the verdict should generally also include a request, in the alternative, for a new trial.

A separate motion for a new trial immediately after the verdict may be made orally. The better practice is to submit such a motion in writing with proper supporting authorities and reference to the record. Such a motion differs from a motion for a directed verdict in that it calls into question issues of both law and fact.

A motion for a new trial should always be considered when the verdict has been contrary to your client's interests. It should not be brought merely as a reflex action, but only when good and sufficient grounds for making the motion exist. The major consideration is whether the client will fare any better the second time around. (Obviously the motion, if granted, serves as a vital settlement negotiation tool.)

In addition to the foregoing, you should utilize motions for a stay of entry of judgment pending appeal (or determination of post-trial motions).

Further Reading

Am. Jur. 2d, Federal Practice and Procedure. Vol. 32. Rochester, NY: Lawyers Cooperative Publishing Co.,

Am. Jur. 2d, New Trial. Vol. 58. Rochester, NY: Lawyers Cooperative Publishing Co.,

Corpus Juris Secundum. Vols. 35A & 35B. St. Paul, Minn.: West Publishing Co.,

Federal Rules of Civil Procedure.,

Goldstein's Trial Technique. Wilmette, Ill.: Callaghan and Co.,

Herr, Haydock, and Stempel. *Motion Practice.* 1985.

Moore's Federal Practice 2d. St. Paul, Minn.: West Publishing,

Motions in Federal Court: Civil Practice. Colorado Springs, Co.: Shephard's McGraw Hill, 1982.

14-1 CHECKLIST OF POST-TRIAL MOTIONS

A. Motions filed after close of evidence.

    1. Motions to correct or perfect the record—"housekeeping" motions.
        a. Motion to strike.
            1) Evidence admitted conditionally and not connected.
            2) Incompetent evidence now apparent.
        b. Motion to amend pleadings to conform to proof—by right.

    2. Motion on the merits. Motion for directed verdict:
        a. Argument must state specific grounds.
        b. Necessary as foundation for motion N.O.V.
        c. N.B.—if both sides move for directed verdict, case is removed from jury.

B. Post-trial motions.

    1. Motion for directed verdict.

    2. Motion to reopen case for additional evidence.

    3. Motion for judgment notwithstanding the verdict.
        a. Prior motion for directed verdict is prerequisite.
        b. Alternative is motion for new trial.

C. Motion for new trial. Grounds (see state rules):

    1. Excessive or inadequate damages.

    2. Fatally defective verdicts.

    3. Verdict contrary to the evidence or against the weight of the evidence.

    4. Jury misconduct.

    5. Newly discovered evidence.

    6. Verdict contrary to law.

    7. Irregularity in the proceedings.

    8. Accident or surprise that could not have been prevented by ordinary prudence.

D. Motion for stay of entry of judgment.

    1. Pending appeal.

    2. Pending disposition of post-trial motions.

14-2 TIMETABLE FOR POST-TRIAL MOTIONS

Federal Rule	State Rule	Type of Motion	Time
50a	_____	Direct verdict	Close of evidence
50b	_____	Renewed JNOV	10 days after entry of judgment
50b	_____	Alternative new trial	Same
56	_____	Summary judgment	After answering and within 10 day before hearing
59	_____	Motion for new trial	10 days after entry of judgment
59c	_____	Alter or amend judgment	10 days after entry of judgment
60a	_____	Relief from judgment	Anytime
60b	_____	Mistake, inadvertence	Within one year of judgment
62b	_____	Stay proceedings to enforce	At judgment

15 | Jury Instructions

I. Introduction

Jury instructions refer to the instructions or "charge" the court gives to the jury on the law at the end of the case (and usually after closing arguments). Different jurisdictions and judges vary in how far they will go beyond a generic recitation of the law-and how much they will discuss the facts of the case. However, all courts allow the lawyers to propose or request instructions and generally conduct a charge conference before closing arguments. You should always view this as a key opportunity to help the judge and the jury understand and appreciate your view of the case and the law. Consult your local rules, other lawyers, and the clerk for the mechanics of submitting requests.

Start early. Jury instructions should be drafted with your closing argument in mind. The language in the instructions, although nonargumentative, should trace the conclusions presented in your opening and closing arguments.

Make sure your proposed charges are supported by the evidence. Prepare alternate charges if there is any question of the admissibility of evidence or objection to the charge itself.

Objections to jury charges can be based on (1) the failure to give a charge or (2) an incorrect charge or (3) a charge that is outside the scope of the pleadings and evidence. The timing of objections is governed by local rules of procedure, either by specific objection at the time of the charge or by general objection to the charges. Finally, there may be an objection to the manner in which the judge delivers the charges.

Consider the use of special verdicts with interrogatories to the jury in cases with complex or technical facts, complex causes or party situations, or extremely emotional fact situations. Carefully draft the interrogatories so that any error or misunderstanding by the jury of the facts or the charges will be apparent from their answers.

II. Preparation of Requests for Instructions

Prepare in advance of trial. View the pleadings in light of instructions, and determine if amendment needed. Determine the evidence needed to support the charges. Prepare during trial—to cover new issues or evidence.

Frame the language of instructions without argument and in simple terms. Use language to marshal factual evidence. Do not assume facts in dispute. Preamble: "If find from evidence . . .," "If find defendant liable and if find plaintiff was injured as proximate result of defendant's act. . . ." Draft language of instructions to follow language in opening and summation.

Form—Use separate, numbered sheets with heading at the top giving subject area, and sources at bottom. Where there may be controversy, prepare several alternate charges. If the court refuses one, propose the second.

III. Objections and Exceptions

Omission—failure to give a charge. Objection must be made at the time of the charge conference, if judge is refusing to give a proposed charge, and/or at the time the charge is given.

Commission—misstating a charge or introducing issue not supported by evidence or pleadings. There is a split of authority. Some jurisdictions hold that no specific objection is needed and a general objection is sufficient, while in some jurisdictions explicit objection is required. You should also consider the tactical questions of objecting to errors of commission: objecting or relying on appeal by you or other side.

Manner of charge—undue emphasis and prejudicial comments. It may be necessary to make an offer of proof to make sure the record includes more than the dry spoken word.

IV. Form of Verdict

Special verdict—Jury answers specific questions on factual issues in dispute. This may be used in the following circumstances:

- complex fact situation with subtle distinctions;

- long economic case;
- multiple parties, claims, and cross claims; and
- strong jury bias or prejudice.

Interrogatories—general verdict with questions. If answers consistent, judge may enter judgment, return case to jury, or order new trial. If answers inconsistent, judge returns case to jury or orders new trial.

Further Reading

Arnold. *Special Verdicts.* 6 Am. Jur. Trials 1043 (1967).

Berdon. *Instructive Interrogatories: Helping the Civil Jury to Understand.* 55 Conn. Bar. J. 179 (January 1981).

Devitt and Blackmar. *Federal Jury Practice and Instruction.* Vol. 1, ch. 6 (3d ed. 1977).

Douthwaite, Graham. *Jury Instructions: Pattern and Otherwise.* 29 Defense L.J. 335 (1980).

McBride. *The Art of Instructing the Jury.* (1969).

Model Jury Instructions: Business Torts Litigation. Chicago: American Bar Association. 1992.

Model Jury Instructions: Employment. Chicago: American Bar Association. 1994.

Model Jury Instructions: Securities. Chicago: American Bar Association. 1996.

Musser. *Instructing the Jury—Pattern Instructions.* 6 Am. Jur. Trials 923 (1967).

Sand, Hon. Leonard B. *Modern Federal Jury Instructions.* New York: Matthew Bender and Co.,

Schweitzer. *Cyclopedia of Trial Practice.* Vol. 1. (2d ed. 1970).

16 | Closing Argument

I. Introduction

Preparation of your closing argument should begin with the initial investigation of the case. Everything you do in furtherance of the case should lead to the conclusions and call to action you will present to the jury in closing. To prepare for this moment, open an Argument file early and fill it with notes, copies of documents, and anything else that might be helpful for your closing argument.

In the investigation and research stage of pretrial preparation, you should have narrowed the issues involved to one or two key issues (no more than three) that form your theory of the case. This theme is the crucial unifying principle of your case, which you want to sell to the jury in closing. Your argument should stress these two or three key points or issues you know you can win. Do not rehash each minute fact, but concentrate on your themes that illustrate the fundamental right and wrong underlying the case. Use your best evidence and demonstrative exhibits admitted during the trial to illustrate points in argument.

The purpose of closing argument is to tie the whole case together. For effective argument, find ways to do this literally, not just figuratively. Plan your opening statement with your closing in mind, then come back to and reference the promises you made in opening, ("when I first had the chance to speak to you in opening statement, I promised . . ."). Conversely, if the other side made the mistake of overstating its case in opening, make them regret it in your closing, ("the defendant's lawyers made you some promises in their opening about what the evidence would show, and you have a right to ask if they've kept their promises . . .").

As plaintiff, you should devote the majority of your final argument to the defendant's wrongdoing and the resulting damages suffered by the plaintiff. As the plaintiff focuses on damages and reparation, the defendant should focus the majority of his argument on liability issues. Plaintiff should anticipate and answer any questions the jury may have on the evidence or credibility of witnesses. Anticipate the defendant's argument on his strong points and rebut them in your closing argument rather than waiting for rebuttal after defendant's presentation. Plan the rebuttal before closing arguments.

One strategy for plaintiff is to develop questions to defendant on your strong points and call for answers, thereby forcing defendant to spend the argument answering your strongest points. Obviously, avoid this tactic if they have good answers. Concentrate on those issues or points where defendant is weakest. Narrow the argument down to your strongest and the defendant's weakest point.

II. General Considerations

Limit closing to key points and reduce it to essential issues (no more than three). Present issues or points that your opponent will have to rebut in his or her argument. Anticipate jury questions regarding conflicting evidence. Use exhibits and transcripts where they are dramatic and effective. For example, transcribe key sections of transcript when critical. Underline key portions to read and show them to the jury.

Personalize the parties and witnesses, highlighting favorable and unfavorable attributes. Discuss the points that attack or support credibility. Remember in a civil case to develop the negative presumptions from the failure of a party to testify or produce evidence under his control.

Use powerful, descriptive catchwords and phrases. Avoid legalese. Use all the tools at your disposal, not just words: change voice and pace, use silence and contrast, use movement and body language. Use demonstrative evidence.

III. Preparation and Delivery

Open Strong

Grab the jury's attention, and deliver your theme once again. Build a personal bridge to the jury. Make them feel important.

- They alone determine party's future.
- Jury is the conscience of the community where defendant is bad or plaintiff unworthy.

- Jury is not made up of individuals but is a body that can stand for something. Refer to age and history of jury tradition.
- Make jury feel like participants in a big case and a great cause.
- Give jury attitude of esteem and prestige from return of big verdict—no achievement to give defendant a verdict.
- Voir dire promises—remind jurors.

Explain burden of proof in real terms not in legalese. Explain preponderance of evidence—probability—and that it depends on the quality of evidence, not quantity. Compare to decisions in everyday life, such as buying a car. Defendant has no burden to show plaintiff wrong; plaintiff has burden to show right. Plaintiff must show more than possibility—clear weight of evidence.

Facts

Define issues. Appeal to logic and common sense. Illustrate with factual pegs or examples for jury to hang on to during discussion. Review uncontested issues first, emphasize how much of your case is "admitted" by the other side. Review your strong points. Summarize the evidence in a narrative sequence, relate testimony to key points, and support the credibility of witnesses. Approach opponent's strong points and your weak points, either by direct attack or confession and avoidance. Anticipate the defendant's arguments. Anticipate and rebut evidence or arguments defendant bound to use. Frame questions to ask defendant so defendant spends time answering. Avoid open-ended questions unless there are no answers. Explain contributory negligence, and related concepts. The slightest degree of fault does not amount to contributory negligence. Use the reasonably prudent man—average man—analogy. For example, a slight error does not keep honor student from Phi Beta Kappa. The courtroom doors are not open only to perfect man; no man free from slightest fault. The plaintiff need not be an A or B student; only a C student.

Cover Injury and Disability

Deal with subjective symptoms or negative tests. Doctors know when a patient is telling the truth. Doctors deal with plaintiff's complaints and description of feelings every day in practice. Only veterinarians and pediatricians use objective findings (and then they ask others). These symptoms actually guide doctor in diagnosis and treatment; it's silly to ask jury to disregard. Doctors admit or explain that X-rays and tests may not always show nonvisible and soft-tissue injuries. Doctors admit broken bones sometimes heal faster than torn muscles, and so on.

Attack defendant's contention that injury *might* be caused by something else. It is not logical. It's just smoke and mirrors. Defendant must show an alternative cause and that it is *more likely* the cause.

Address a prior condition—aggravation or precipitation. Prior condition caused plaintiff no problems prior to injury. Defendant takes plaintiff as he finds him—egg and steel analogy; or antique statues of lead, glass, and wood.

Call for Action—What to Do and Why.

Dramatize the benefits of plaintiff's verdict—impact on defendant. For example:

- Prevent repetition / deter others.
- Promote safer products.
- Encourage better warnings, inspections, care.
- Defendant's verdict rewards conduct.
- Stress plaintiff's innocence and defendant's callousness.
- Consumer protection—plaintiff was seeking service or product, not lifetime of pain or disability.

Damages

Explain or define pain and suffering. Analogies:

- State cannot inflict pain on criminals (cruel and unusual punishment).
- Pain is opposite of pleasure and comfort.
- We all spend money for pleasures or comfort or to avoid pain (dentists).
- There is no cure for pain.

Explain compensatory damages. Jurors only can decide damages; witness cannot express. Compare condemnation case or replacing loss of an object, such as race horse, versus award for pain or disability for loss of good health. Plaintiff only wants damages for what was taken away from him. List things and activities lost to plaintiff by injury; defendant took away and replaced with pain. No sympathy or charity; just full and fair compensation. Entitled to full damages—no more and no less. If entitled to $10,000, then $9,000 means $9,000 worth of justice and $1,000 worth of injustice.

Determine whether to ask the jury for a specific amount. Use per diem approach, or other formula for damages.

- Physical pain and suffering: $____ per day for ____mos./yrs. = _____.
- Mental anguish and suffering: $____ per day for ____mos./yrs. = _____.
- Loss of past earnings: $____ per mo./yr. = _____.
- Loss of future earning capacity: $____ per yr. for ____yrs. = _____.
- Loss of enjoyment of life (whole person): $____ per day for____ mos./yrs. = _____.
- Special damages: $____.
- Total Damages: $____.

Punitive Damages

The drama of punitive damages can take up much of your argument. Stress the social purpose of punitive award. Show consequences of not punishing defendant. Admit that the award is windfall to plaintiff, but deserved based on heinous nature of conduct. Refusing punitive damages is a windfall for the defendant.

Close Strong

Return to your themes, thank the jury, and ask for the right result.

Further Reading

Smith, Lawrence J. *Art of Advocacy—Summation*. New York: Matthew Bender and Co.

Stein, Jacob. *Closing Argument*. Wilmette, Ill.: Callaghan and Co.

Tigar, Michael E. *Persuasion: The Litigator's Art*. Chicago: American Bar Association, 1999.

About the Editor

DANIEL I. SMALL is a trial lawyer with the Boston, Massachusetts, law firm of Butters, Brazilian & Small. His practice focuses on SEC and other government agency investigations, complex civil litigation, selected white-collar criminal matter, Qui Tam, and general healthcare law. Previously, Mr. Small was Vice President of Legal Affairs and General Counsel of InPhyNet Medical Management Inc., a national publicly traded healthcare staffing and management firm doing business in twenty-five states. Prior to that, Mr. Small was counsel to the Boston law firm of Widett, Slate and Goldman; an Assistant U.S. Attorney in Boston, and a Trial Attorney with the Criminal Division of the U.S.Department of Justice. Mr. Small is author of *Preparing Witnesses* (American Bar Association, 1998). He is chair of the ABA Criminal Justice Section White Collar Crime Committee.

Mr. Small was a Lecturer on Law at Harvard Law School teaching the "Federal Litigation" course, and has taught trial advocacy and other subjects at Harvard, several other law schools, and various continuing legal education programs. He is an Arbitrator for the American Arbitration Association and the NHLA. He is a Contributing Editor to *Covenants Not To Compete*, the ABA Survey, and has had articles published in *The National Law Journal, Miami Herald, Boston Globe, Boston Herald, Massachusetts Lawyers Weekly, Medical Business, Boston Business Journal, Mass. High Tech,* and *Salem Evening News.* He is also a frequent TV and online commentator for MSNBC.com.

About the Contributors

KARL BECKMEYER is a member of the firm Beckmeyer & Mulick in Islamorada, Florida, where he is engaged in a civil trial practice with emphasis on personal injury and commercial litigation. He has written and lectured on trial practice for various state and national seminars and publications. A graduate of the University of Florida Law School, he is a member of the American, Florida, Illinois, and Florida Keys Bar Associations; the Association of Trial Lawyers of America; and a former member of the Florida Bar Board of Governors.

MARJORIE CROWDER BRIGGS is a member of the firm of Porter, Wright, Morris & Arthur in Columbus, Ohio, where she is engaged in a civil trial practice dealing primarily with commercial, business, and insurance coverage litigation. She has written and lectured on trial practice for both state and national seminars and publications. A graduate of The Ohio State University Law School, she is a member of the American, Ohio, and Columbus Bar Associations, and the Defense Research Institute.

STEPHEN C. BUSER is in solo practice in Columbia, Illinois. He specializes in personal injury and civil litigation. He is the Editor-in-Chief of the Illinois Bar Journal (1998-2000), and has authored articles on trial practice for various state and national publications. A graduate of St. Louis University Law School, he is a member of the American and Illinois Bar Associations, and the Association of Trial Lawyers of America.

R. CARL CANNON is a managing member of the firm of Constangy, Brooks, and Smith, L.L.C., in Atlanta, Georgia, where he is engaged in civil trial practice dealing exclusively with employment-related litigation. He has written and lectured on trial practice for both state and national seminars and publications. A graduate of the University of Georgia Law School with an LL.M. from the University of Virginia Law School, he is a member of the American, Georgia, and Atlanta Bar Associations.

G. WARE CORNELL, JR., practices in Fort Lauderdale, Florida, where he is engaged in civil trial practice with emphasis on employment discrimination cases. He has lectured on trial practice for the Federal Bar Association. A graduate of the University of Georgia Law School, he is a member of the American, Florida, and Georgia Bar Associations, and Board Certified Civil Trial Lawyer by the Florida Bar.

CAMERON C. GAMBLE is a sole practitioner in New Orleans, Louisiana, where he is engaged in a civil trial practice dealing primarily with personal injury and wrongful death cases. He has written and lectured on trial practice for various state and national seminars and publications. A graduate of Tulane University Law School, he is a member of the American, Louisiana, and New Orleans Bar Associations. He is a former chair of the ABA General Practice Section, the ABA Standing Committee on Solo and Small Firms, and former President of the New Orleans Bar Association.

STEPHEN KELLY is Vice President and General Counsel for Today.com, Inc., a web development software company in Tempe, Arizona. Previously, he was employed as in-house counsel at Motorola, Inc., Datapoint Corporation, and Fujitsu Business Communication Systems. A graduate of Drake University Law School, he is a member of the Arizona, Illinois, and Maricopa County Bar Associations.

KEVIN M. MYLES is a member of Myles & Myles in Portland, Oregon, where he is engaged in civil trail practice with an emphasis on contract, business, and employment litigation. He has been an adjunct professor at Northwestern School of Law at Lewis and Clark College in government contracts and an instructor at the College of Lake County in business law. A graduate of the University of Illinois College of Law, he is a member of the Oregon, Washington, Multnomah, and Clark County Bar Associations, as well as the Oregon Trial Lawyers Association.

WILLIAM J. O'CONNOR II is a member of the firm of O'Connor & O'Connor, P.C., in Billings Montana, where he is engaged in a civil trial practice with emphasis on personal injury, business litigation, and labor law. He has written and lectured on trial practice for various state and national seminars and publications. A graduate of The Catholic University of America Law School, he is a member of the American, Montana, District of Columbia, and Yellowstone County Bar Associations.

DENNIS L. PETERSON is a member of the firm of Peterson, Fishman, Livgard & Capistrant, P.L.L.P., in Minneapolis, Minnesota, where he is engaged in a civil trial practice dealing primarily with business litigation. A graduate of William Mitchell College of Law, he is a member of the American, Minnesota, and Hennepin County Bar Associations; and the Minnesota Trial Lawyers Association.

JOHN T. PHIPPS is a sole practitioner in Champaign, Illinois, where he is engaged in a civil trial practice dealing primarily with complex civil litigation. He has written and lectured on trial practice for various state and national seminars and publications. A graduate of the University of Illinois, he is a member of the American, Illinois, and Champaign County Bar Associations; the Association of Trial Lawyers of America; and the Illinois Trial Lawyers Association.

JILL A. SMITH is Vice President and Associate Counsel for Key Corp., a bank holding company with assets of approximately $80 billion. A graduate of The Ohio State University Law School, she is a member of the Ohio and Cleveland Bar Associations

ROBERT A. WOODKE is a managing partner in the firm of Brouse, Woodke & Meyer, P.L.L.P., in Bemidji, Minnesota, where he is engaged in a civil trial practice dealing primarily with personal injury, commercial disputes, and the defense of product liability cases. He has written and lectured on trial practice for various state and national seminars and publications. A graduate of Creighton University Law School, he is a member of the Minnesota State Bar Association and past chair of their General Practice, Solo and Small Firm Section. He is a member of the American Bar Association, the past president of the 15th District Bar Association and the Beltrami County Bar Association, and a member of the Minnesota Trial Lawyers Association.

Index

CD
Diskette to accompany
Going to Trial, 2nd edition

What do the diskettes contain?

The 3½" diskette, formatted for PC, contains 60 text (Microsoft Word 6.0) files. The filenames correspond to the 60 numbered forms in *Going to Trial, 2nd edition.*

What hardware and software must I have to use this diskette?

IBM PC or compatible computer with a 3½" high density (1.44 Mb) floppy disk drive, and word processing software.

How should I use these files?

If you plan to use these documents frequently, we recommend that you copy them to a hard disk drive, placing them in a separate directory or folder. To copy the files on a diskette to a hard drive, do the following:

in DOS, use the MS-DOS COPY command to copy all or selected files. For example, COPY A*.* C: copies all the files from the diskette in drive A: to the hard drive.

in Windows, open the 3½" drive A: and select the files you wish to copy. Use the Copy command or drag the icons to the destination folder.

To open the files, use the Open File command in your word processing software to identify the file(s) you wish to use.

Difficulties?

We are not equipped to provide help with specific software problems. If you encounter problems with the disk you received in this package, please call our production department at 312-988-6065.

CD FOR THIS BOOK IS LOCATED AT THE CIRCULATION DESK.
PLEASE INQUIRE AT THE DESK FOR CHECKOUT.

CD

Diskette to accompany
Going to Trial, 2nd edition

WARNING: Removing the disk from its pocket indicates your understanding and acceptance of the following Terms and Conditions.

Read the following terms and conditions before removing the disk from its pocket. If you do not agree with them, promptly return this product to the party from whom it was acquired or to the American Bar Association and your money will be returned.

The document files on this diskette are a proprietary product of the American Bar Association and are protected by Copyright Law. The American Bar Association retains title to and ownership of these files.

License

You may use this set of files on a single computer or move it to and use it on another computer, but under no circumstances may you use the set of files on more than one computer at the same time. You may copy the diskette either in support of your use of the files on a single computer or for backup purposes.

You may permanently transfer the set of files to another party if the other party agrees to accept the terms and conditions of this License Agreement. If you transfer the set of files, you must at the same time transfer all copies of the files to the same party or destroy those not transferred. Such transfer terminates your license. You may not rent, lease, assign or otherwise transfer the files except as stated in this paragraph.

You may modify these files for your own use within the provisons of this License Agreement. You may not redistribute any modified files.

Warranty

If a diskette in this package is defective, the American Bar Association will replace it at no charge if the defective diskette is returned to the American Bar Association within 60 days from the date of acquisition.

American Bar Association warrants that these files will perform in substantial compliance with the documentation supplied with this product. However, the American Bar Association does not warrant these forms as to the correctness of the legal material contained therein. If you report a significant defect in performance in writing to the American Bar Association, and the American Bar Association is not able to correct it within 60 days, you may return the diskette, including all copies and documentation, to the American Bar Association and the American Bar Associaton will refund your money.

Any files that you modify will no longer be covered under this warranty even if they were modified in accordance with the License Agreement and product documentation.

In no event will the American Bar Association, its officers, members, or employees be liable to you for any damages, including lost profits, lost savings or other incidental or consequential damages arising out of your use or inability to use these files even if the American Bar Association or an authorized American Bar Association representative has been advised of the possibility of such damages, or for any claim by any other party. Some states do not allow the limitation or exclusion of liability for incidental or consequential damages, in which case this limitation may not apply to you.